GEORGE WASHINGTON'S WOMEN:

Mary, Martha, Sally, and 146 Others

by

George W. Nordham

DORRANCE & COMPANY • *Philadelphia and Ardmore, Pa.*

To Florence, Martha, Diane, Elizabeth, Jeanette, Marian, Jean and Dorothea—important women to me.

Contents

Preface

One of George Washington's best male friends, Lord Fairfax (who was Sally's father) sounded an early warning to all girls and young ladies in Virginia. He looked at Washington at age sixteen and said: "George Washington is beginning to feel the sap rising, being in the spring of life, and is getting ready to be the prey of your sex, wherefor may the Lord help him. . . ."

And prey he did, with wit at times. He commented on a dancing assembly that it was a delight for any woman, just what women liked to see, because in attendance was "one more man" than the number of women.

Washington's efforts to please the ladies occasionally met with sharp rebuke. At a dinner party in 1779, Mrs. George Olney said to him, "If you don't let go of my hand, sir, I'll tear out your eyes and the hair from your head, even if you are a general."

Late in life George Washington rebelled at the prospect of another adult woman moving into his household. He asserted that his firm, unalterable, position was that "never again shall I have two women in my house when I am there myself."

A charmer of women, George Washington was. He was also a realist and an honest man concerning women.

Introduction

George Washington was a busy man. The sketchiest look at his life shows how extremely busy he was. His time was mostly spent in masculine activities: farming, hunting, soldiering, politicking.

But his life included women. Oh, how his life included women! This book considers the most influential women in Washington's life, those women who were a meaningful, significant factor in his daily personal thoughts, women who influenced his character and who left a deep impression on him. It examines his relationship with:

> His mother.
> His wife.
> His stepdaughter.
> His step-granddaughters.
> His first romantic flame.
> The girl he proposed to twice.
> Another girl he could not decide about until it was too late.
> His favorite adult female companion.
> The lady who was his greatest and most passionate love.

It also examines George Washington's attitude toward women in general. And it faces head-on the impact of his sterility, a state that affected materially his relationship with women throughout his life.

Noted biographer James Thomas Flexner said that just as northerners play the game of "George Washington Slept Here," so southerners play the game "My Ancestress Refused George Washington's Offer of Marriage." A comedian quipped: Let's bring the North and South together and play George Washington Slept with My Ancestress and Proposed Marriage Here. This book does not play any of those three games!

The author of this book uses the latest reliable information to assess the important relationships George Washington had with women at all periods of his life. The interpretations are based on serious, objective, intensive research into numerous, respected reference sources. These sources are listed in the bibliography.

When a statement is made that appears harsh and somewhat ungentlemanly, it is made because the writer reached the ultimate conclusion that the facts justified it. And when a statement is seen that appears somewhat flowery, again it is made because the writer decided the circumstances could best be described by such language. Accuracy has been the constant goal; let the chips fall as they may as the unfolding facts show various patterns.

The writer entered this effort with a totally open mind about George Washington's women. Wherever the authoritative information led, that path was followed to see how it was pertinent to the subject matter.

The walk was fascinating to take. I hope you find my presentation of it equally rewarding. The women you will meet are sure to be as interesting to you as they were to me, and to George Washington.

George Washington's Attitude
Toward Women in General

As AN ELIGIBLE bachelor, George Washington was awkward with women. His approach toward them was too hesistant, too shy.

As a married adult, he was "utterly charming." His attitude toward women had matured considerably.

He treated women with deference. He was gracious, gallant, and gentlemanly toward them; and he was also shy, restrained, reticent.

Until his marriage at age twenty-six, George Washington was no ladies' man. He did not do well with girls and young ladies. Biographers say he was lacking in too many aspects. He lacked free and easy speech; his mind and tongue were too slow. He lacked surface vivacity; he lacked quick and spontaneous humor. He lacked the air of a confident, fun-loving person. He lacked family female inspiration.

After his marriage he continued to lack mostly what he had lacked before. Only now he was a ladies' man. He did very well with adult women. Biographers say he did so well because women were attracted and charmed by his prominent status in the army and in the new federal government; by his flattery (he had the ability to associate name and face and then have total immediate recall at future meetings); by his genuine fondness of female company; and by his thoughtfulness toward women.

Washington, at age fifty-one, wrote to Mrs. Richard Stockton, a lady poet from New Jersey, that: "When once the woman has tempted us and we have tasted the forbidden fruit, there is no such thing as checking our appetites, whatever the consequences may be.''

And at age sixty-six, he told his step-granddaughter, Betey Custis, that a marriage partner should possess good sense, good disposition, good reputation, and financial means.

Washington liked his "quiet wife, a quiet soul." He spoke affectionately of "domestic felicity," of tranquility, of how Martha Washington was an "agreeable consort for life." His attitude toward his private, personal woman was not the same as it was for women generally. Usually he liked lively, vivacious women with quick minds.

George Washington was no prude. He spoke of sexual passion, of adultery, and of "giddy rounds of promiscuous pleasure." His youthful friends are reported to have called him the "stallion of the Potomac." His huge body, six feet two, 175 pounds, muscular, athletic, well formed and well developed, surely had to be physically attractive to women. Washington would question proposed new officers for the army about their drinking habits, but never about their women, their sex life. He would tell his step-granddaughter of the virtues of love and marriage but would never mention sexual purity.

Washington thoroughly enjoyed dances. It is said that he enjoyed the physical pleasure of rhythmic movement, the faster the beat, the better. He also enjoyed the social intercourse with women at dances and parties. In 1775 he was at The Hermitage, located in what is now Hohokus, New Jersey. There "at Mrs. Prevost's we talked and walked and laughed and danced and gallanted away the leisure hours.''

His personal diary records his thoughts about the number and appearance of women at a series of nine social events, within about one month. These events were part of his southern tour as first president of the United States:

April 21, 1791——the company at the dancing assembly in Newbern, North Carolina included "about seventy ladies."
May 3, 1791——was visited by a "great number of the most respectable ladies of Charleston," (South Carolina). He found it "flattering."

May 4, 1791——"went to a very elegant dancing assembly at which there were 256 elegantly dressed and handsome women."

May 5, 1791——". . . there were at least 400 ladies, the number and appearance of which exceeded any thing of the kind I had ever seen."

May 6, 1791——". . . went to a Ball in the evening where there was a select company of ladies."

May 13, 1791——". . . went to a dancing assembly at which there were about 100 well-dressed and handsome ladies." This was at Puryeburg, South Carolina.

May 18, 1791——". . . drank Tea with many well dressed ladies."

May 19, 1791——"went to an assembly at which there were between 60 and 70 well dressed ladies." This was in Augusta, Georgia.

May 23, 1791——". . . dined with a number of Gentlemen and Ladies . . . round about to the amount of 150, of which 50 or 60 were of the latter."

During his prime years, Washington moved into a room or onto a dance floor with ease and sureness, creating an imposing sight. He moved with grace and dignity. His physical presence seemed to excite gatherings, and his person seemed to dominate the area.

One of his moving emotional experiences with women in general took place near Trenton, New Jersey, in April, 1789. Rows of matrons and girls of all ages lined his route, and a chorus of white-robed young ladies sang a song of welcome to him, while smaller girls spread freshly cut flowers in his path. President-elect George Washington, on his way to the inauguration in New York City, was "visibly moved." He thanked them and that night took the time to write to "The Ladies of Trenton who assembled at the Triumphal Arch." He expressed his appreciation for the "novel and grateful manner" in which they honored him. It was a most "exquisite sensation." No wonder George Washington was utterly charming to the ladies! His feats and prominence and presence inspired them, and then he himself made sure they realized how much he appreciated it all.

One example of Washington's attitude toward women in general is seen in his handling of Peggy Shippen, the young bride of Benedict Arnold. She told Washington she was not involved in any way in her husband's treason. Washington did not question her statement. He accepted it and therefore did not even consider punishment for her. He merely arranged for her prompt return to her father in Philadelphia. Other officers wanted to handle it differently, but George Washington completely accepted the lady's word of honor.

George Washington relished the company of lively, vivacious, fashionable women. He could not easily resist them. It has been said that "this man had the blood of a lover." And at one ball he attended "his eyes were perpetually roaming over the ladies."

As Washington matured, he was a ladies' man because his attitude toward them was what they wanted in those colonial days. He was respectful, deferential, courteous, restrained. Washington was utterly charming to women in general because he found alert, active women utterly charming too.

The name of George Washington has a lasting charm for women. Today two organizations in particular continue to pay tribute to the memory of this attractive man. The National Society of the Daughters of the American Revolution was formed to further the memory and spirit of those patriots, ancestors, who achieved American independence. The society works in numerous ways, with dedication and effectiveness, to preserve the freedoms Americans cherish. And the Mount Vernon Ladies Association of the Union overcame every imaginable obstacle, in their dedicated efforts to preserve Washington's home. This group of women struggled financially, politically, and in virtually every other way, to finally become the owners of Mount Vernon by contract signed on April 6, 1958. They lovingly restored it, faithful to the original appearance, and followed the urgings of their first leader, Miss Ann Pamela Cunningham, who told them: "Those who go to the home in which he lived and died wish to see in what he lived and died."

George Washington's attitude toward women in general was positive; he liked them. And likewise, women generally found him utterly charming. They reciprocated with a most complimentary attitude.

2

Frances Alexander

THE YEAR WAS 1748. George Washington was sixteen years old. He was in love. The object of his love, however, is not all that clear. It was either Frances Alexander or it was the idea of love itself.

George Washington, at sixteen, was a big, strapping, muscular young man. He was then taking dancing lessons and beginning to learn the social graces needed in the company of women. But it was a long, slow process, and he still felt quite awkward about women and was uncomfortable in mixed company. George also was a slow and deliberate thinker, one who did not find it easy to make small talk or to flirt with young women.

So, he turned to writing his innermost romantic thoughts. His known relationship with Frances Alexander produced three items of George Washington's romantic writing efforts. Surely, he was trying to say what was in his heart about her, but it had to be in writing because his tongue just wasn't that facile.

The first item was a piece of verse, an acrostic in honor of Frances Alexander, which Washington wrote in 1748. It reads in full as follows:

> From your bright sparkling eyes I was undone;
> Rays you have more transparent than the sun,
> Amidst its glory in the rising Day,
> None can you equal in your bright array;
> Constant in your calm and unspotted Mind,
> Equal to all, but will to none prove kind;
> So, knowing, seldom one so young, you'll find
> Ah! woe's me, that I should love and conceal,

5

> Long have I wished, but never dare reveal,
> Even tho severely love's pains I feel;
> Xerxes that great, wasn't free from Cupid's Dart,
> And all the greatest Heros [sic], felt the smart.

George Washington followed that acrostic with a poem, a sonnet to Frances Alexander, also written in 1748. It reads in full as follows:

> Oh Ye Gods why should my poor resistless heart
> Stand to oppose thy might and power
> At last surrender to cupid's feathered dart
> And now lays bleeding every hour
> For her that's pitiless of my grief and woes
> And will not on me pity take
> I'll sleep amongst my most inveterate foes
> And with gladness never (wish) to wake
> In deluding sleepings let my eyelids close
> That in an enraptured dream I may
> In a soft lulling sleep and gentle repose
> Possess those joys denied by Day.

The third romantic item Goerge Washington wrote to or about Frances Alexander is contained in a letter to his boy friend, Robin. At the time he wrote it, Washington was living at the home of William Fairfax and was most impressed with Fairfax's daughter, Sally. In 1748 George Washington took pen in hand and wrote to Robin that by seeing Sally virtually every day it "brings the other into my remembrance." And it "revives my former passion for your Low Land Beauty." But then George's hesitancy became evident as he wrote that "were I ever to attempt anything, I should only get a denial which would be only adding grief to uneasiness." George Washington, at sixteen, was not prepared and not ready for another assault on his heart. Somewhat philosophically, he continued that such a new assault on his heart "cannot be more fierce than it has been."

Certainly, George Washington was a romantic soul at the tender age of sixteen. His references to Cupid and the "feathered dart" show just how romantic were his dreams and thoughts at that period of his life.

6

The identity of the "Low Land Beauty" has caused considerable guessing over the years. The latest and most reliable evidence convinces this writer that Frances Alexander was the Low Land Beauty to whom George Washington was referring. Other writers and biographers have decided that the Beauty may have been any one of a number of girls who were nearby neighbors. Jane Strother is one name that appears as a candidate; Lucy Grymes is another candidate and Mary Cary is yet another. The names Ann Carol and Mary McDaniel also appear. These two young ladies were charged with stealing George Washington's clothes while he was swimming in the river. Ann was found innocent and discharged. Mary was found guilty of petty larceny and punished by fifteen lashes across her bare back. Because the legal action took place in 1751, it seems unlikely that either of these two pranksters were the Low Land Beauty.

Writers in the late 1800s tended to settle most frequently on the name Mary Bland as being the real Low Land Beauty. Mary Bland lived in Westmoreland and has been described as George Washington's "love" when he was age fourteen. More recent writers have answered the question, "Who was the Low Land Beauty?" by saying who it could *not* be. Thus, Betsy Fauntleroy is ruled out by the date of Washington's letter, her age at that time, and his age at that time. Sally Fairfax has also been ruled out by the wording of Washington's letter itself. It makes no sense if you read the letter with the name Sally Fairfax substituted for the phrase "Low Land Beauty." And two biographers have answered that question with candor. Rupert Hughes declared flatly: "Nobody knows." James Thomas Flexner stated, "she has been so widely identified that she has more heads than Cerberus."

Within a short time after Washington wrote both the acrostic in honor of Frances Alexander and the sonnet to Frances Alexander, he wrote no more. Biographers interpret this cessation of display of romantic emotion to mean that either (a) George grew out of his period of romantic love itself, or (b) he grew tired of the charms of Frances Alexander.

In either case, George no longer saw or referred to Frances

Alexander. His first affair of the heart, at age sixteen, was over and done with. Probably it left a few small scars. He seemed to have indeed been taken by the experience.

3

Betsy Fauntleroy

GEORGE WASHINGTON proposed marriage to Betsy Fauntleroy twice. Twice he was rejected.

George had gotten over his sixteen-year-old's penchant for romanticizing about Frances Alexander. He was now twenty years old. He had been around in social circles more and was more relaxed in female company. Maybe he now was also more realistic in defining his wants about the woman he sought to be his wife.

Betsy Fauntleroy was sixteen years old when George Washington wooed her. She was the daughter of Washington's neighbor, William Fauntleroy, a wealthy man of high social standing in Virginia. Betsy was a small young lady. She had a round, petite face with brunette hair and brown eyes. Her slightly turned-up nose and smiling lips were suggestive of her pixy nature. She was a vivacious, spirited girl with a fine social background and plenty of exposure to social graces. She had many charming features.

Biographers, however, have questioned whether George Washington was taken by Betsy Fauntleroy's charms or by her worldly possessions. He clearly was impressed by her solid social standing and knowledgeable ways. He also knew very well the influence and power of her rich father. It might be just the combination for the kind of match he needed to gain firmer acceptance in Virginia social circles.

So, George Washington pursued Betsy Fauntleroy with considerable vigor and openness. His first proposal of marriage apparently was made shortly before he left on a trip. Little is known

9

of his full reactions to her rejection. Being miles away and busy with other thoughts probably helped divert his attention and ease the pain of rejection.

On his return he began again to woo her. This time he turned his attention to Betsy Fauntleroy in the accepted custom of the times. He wrote to her father.

In fact, George Washington wrote two letters in the summer of 1752. The letter to Betsy's father asked permission to visit and call on Miss Betsy "in the hopes of a revocation of the former cruel sentence and see if I can meet with any alteration in my favor." George enclosed a sealed letter addressed to Betsy and asked her father to give it to her. That letter to Betsy has not been found and apparently is lost to history. It is said to have contained another proposal of marriage.

In any event, Betsy Fauntleroy rejected George Washington's attention in no uncertain terms. The rejection was so strong and definite that George withdrew from any further efforts to win Betsy Fauntleroy. Her name never again appears in any of George Washington's correspondence or other papers. In her mind, it was a closed chapter, and he accepted the finality of her decision.

The best indications in known sources suggest that George Washington's proposals of marriage to Betsy Fauntleroy never got very far. They met with the instant and strong disapproval of her father. William Fauntleroy found George Washington an unacceptable suitor for his daughter. The Washington family did not measure up to his expectations for his daughter's future life. He considered them a "secondary" family. William Fauntleroy also considered the Washington farm and property as "second-rate." And to nail the coffin to this romance completely shut, Mr. Fauntleroy said that George Washington, despite his huge size and powerful build, seemed to be a "sickly" young man, too often prone to attacks of ague and pleurisy and similar ailments, and a man with a mouthful of horrible teeth. Mr. Fauntleroy found intolerable the idea that becoming a nursemaid would be his daughter's lot in life.

With such strongly adverse feelings of her father, it left little for sixteen-year-old Betsy Fauntleroy to think about. At that period of time, girls did marry at age fourteen or fifteen or sixteen, but virtually never without the wholehearted support and blessings of her own family. In certain circumstances, lukewarm support might be overcome by a young suitor, but rarely, and especially among families of good social standing, was it possible to change totally negative family reactions.

Thus George Washington's first serious love affair with someone he wanted to marry ended in complete rejection. He never again took up the pursuit of Betsy Fauntleroy.

4

Mary Eliza Philipse

MARY ELIZA PHILIPSE was born on July 3, 1730. George Washington was twenty-four years old when he met her in 1756, when she was almost twenty-six years old.

George had four years earlier proposed marriage to the brown-eyed, brunette beauty, Betsy Fauntleroy. Now he was courting Mary Eliza Philipse, also a brown-eyed, brunette beauty. The physical attraction of George Washington to Mary Eliza Philipse is well documented and clearly in evidence.

Her posture was erect. She had clear and confident eyes, a rather large nose, and a full mouth, which was firm and sensuous with small dimples at both corners. She was slim, beautiful, and statuesque. On her neck a swelling showed that appears to have been a goiter.

To a man of George's age, twenty-four, the mental maturing process was in full evidence. Gone were the romantic love ideas which were so strongly in evidence when George was sixteen years old. Then he was writing love verse and poetry to Frances Alexander. Those fantasies were now replaced by a realistic search for an attractive companion for himself for life, and a mother for his planned and hoped-for children. George Washington himself commented about Mary Eliza Philipse that she was "deep-bosomed" and "likely to produce healthy and vigorous children." This seemed to be of major importance to Washington in his quest for a life partner at that time.

Mary Eliza Philipse's beauty was widely acknowledged. But her personality was also a powerful factor in the total picture. It had several interesting aspects to it.

First was her gaiety and sophistication. It earned her the fond nickname "Polly." Polly Philipse was a well-bred, metropolitan woman, one quite unaccustomed to a farmer's view of things.

She was also sincere and interesting. George Washington said Polly was forthright of speech, which inspired "confidence in her intelligence and her sincerity." George's mind continued to be slow and his speech not fluent and easy. He pondered the correct thing to say; from Polly the right words flowed easily.

A third facet of Polly's personality was her strong will. It was a well-known and dominant trait. It has been called a "notorious" strong will. It was so strong a characteristic of her that several historians say it is the principal reason she still was single at age twenty-six. In colonial America, Polly Philipse was definitely considered a spinster by reaching age twenty-six without a marriage.

Polly Philipse's nature was to dominate other people. She was rich and beautiful and knowledgeable, so she had immense influence over everyone, older persons as well as her peers. She exercised this influence to the fullest extent and, combined with her powerfully strong will, the overall impact was overwhelming to many persons. She intimidated them. They often retreated before beginning to commit themselves to getting to know her as a complete person. She seemed to make people feel somewhat inadequate. And so at age twenty-six she was still alone in life.

Polly Philipse was already rich when George Washington met and courted her. She then owned 51,000 acres of land in New York. And she also was the natural heiress to great family wealth and even more acreage.

George Washington met Polly Philipse in New York City in February, 1756. He was a house guest at the home of Beverly Robinson, who was the son of John Robinson, Speaker of the Virginia House of Burgesses. Beverly's sister was Polly Philipse. She lived at the house and became a willing companion for Washington on sightseeing tours of New York, and dances and other social functions.

George took Polly to a dance at Mrs. Baron's. And twice he took her to see the Microcosm—"The World in Miniature." This was a colossal show, featuring a machine of 1,200 wheels and pinions, which were simultaneously set into motion. The World was built in the form of a Roman temple by Mr. Henry Bridges of London, who labored for twenty-two years on it. The Roman temple setting was lavish with sculptures and other eye-catching and dazzling ideas. Polly's sophistication took the Microcosm in stride; George was awed by it all.

George's courting efforts were encouraged by mutual friends. But, alas, Polly Philipse found that while Colonel George Washington may have been a good soldier, he was "not a lover."

Apparently, George never proposed marriage to Polly. He was still trying to make up his mind about doing that when Polly announced her engagement to Roger Morris. Washington realized that any decision on his part was just too late.

Was George Washington hurt by Polly's announcement? Probably not too much. He may have had a slightly wounded heart and maybe wondered about his own delays in the affair. She had taken his fancy, but only for a relatively brief period of time. He accepted the news of her planned marriage to Mr. Morris quite easily. George had been very hesitant in his relationship with Polly. His efforts to win her and perhaps propose marriage to her have been described by writers as "half-hearted."

The best evidence indicates that George Washington saw in Polly Philipse's personality too much of his own mother's domineering and stubbornly strong will. The thought of a lifelong togetherness under this influence, after having already had it for his childhood, was too much to accept quickly. Instead of a dream, George may have seen a nightmare ahead.

So, with all Polly Philipse's beauty, physical charms, social graces, and wealth, her personality did not strike George Washington right. He did not really seek her hand with unquestioning aggression. He lingered and was indecisive about the whole situation. And when, and if, he was ready to make a positive move toward her, she was already gone to someone else.

Polly probably shared the feeling that their relationship was not exactly right. She did not concentrate all her time and attention on this one suitor; she saw George Washington, but she saw other men too.

The powerful, adverse reactions of Betsy Fauntleroy's father to George Washington's proposals of marriage to his daughter in 1752 were not duplicated in George's relationship with Polly Philipse. There is no evidence that Polly's father found a possible match with Washington objectionable. This time the decision was made by the parties themselves; or, perhaps more accurately, the parties never reached the point of having to make a decision about marrying each other.

Less than one month after Polly Philipse announced her engagement to Mr. Morris, George Washington met Martha Dandridge Custis, who was to become the one and only Mrs. George Washington.

5

Sarah Cary Fairfax

SARAH CARY FAIRFAX (Sally) had the most influence of any woman on George Washington's life. She taught him, required him, virtually *forced* him, to develop and maintain one of his finest traits—the ability to curb his emotions, to restrain his passions, to quietly accept facts instead of dreams.

She was the power behind his lifelong total sense of reality. This proved necessary and invaluable while he calmly and dispassionately led the makeshift armies to victory against seemingly overwhelming odds. It was essential and priceless while he led, with quiet dignity, great reserve, and a "cool" head, the insecure and untested new form of federal government, when he would have preferred to spend those latter years of his life at his Mount Vernon plantation.

Sally Fairfax was George Washington's greatest, longest-lasting, most passionate, and most significant love. His early, guilt-ridden, doomed, traumatic experiences with her brought, on balance in the long run, more sorrow than joy. But they also helped greatly to make him into a real man.

Sally was the most fascinating woman George Washington ever knew. She was also the most baffling to him. She forever kept him off-balance about their emotional relationship. Sally was a flirt to George: a lady who encouraged, discouraged, re-encouraged, then ignored him over and over again. She frustrated and puzzled him more fully than any other female he ever knew.

It was to Sally Fairfax that George Washington wrote openly at age twenty-six of his love for her and pleadingly asked her for some expression that she felt the same toward him. The expression was not contained in her reply. So George wrote back with hurt and bewilderment, "Do we still misunderstand the true meaning of each other's letters?"

And it was also to Sally Fairfax that George Washington wrote, at age sixty-six, less than two years before his death, wondering why she did not come back to Virginia and "spend the evening of your life" down the road from Mount Vernon.

And it was the name of Sally Fairfax that appears in George Washington's personal diary entries as a neighbor at whose home he dined and was entertained—these were the only such visits he thought "important" enough during twenty years to note the hostess's name in his personal book of memorable records. He visited her home thirty-seven times just in the one five-year period between 1768 and 1773.

Noted biographer James Thomas Flexner looked closely at the Sally Fairfax/George Washington relationship over the years. He said, ". . . the exact nature of their relationship cannot be defined." Other writers have concluded that Sally Fairfax is "interesting because George Washington found her so." And still others say the early relationship was a pure, romantic one between two young people who were not ashamed to remain close and good friends long after the fires dwindled. It had a "melancholy beauty" in it.

George Washington fell in love with the wife of his neighbor and his own best friend. He was guilty about that feeling. And so he tried to hide it by saying it was really Sally's sister, Mary, who attracted him. He indicated that he had continuing and major business to conduct with Sally's husband and that the repeated visits to her home, Belvoir, were prompted by things other than Sally Fairfax. This attempted ploy is in repeated evidence for ten years, until 1758, when George Washington finally confessed in no uncertain or misleading words that he loved Sally Fairfax.

Before she was married, George Washington did not know Sally Cary. He never met her until after she had become Mrs. Sally Fairfax. He was then sixteen years old and she was eighteen. He was still in the throes of writing romantic verse and poetry to and about Frances Alexander.

Sally Fairfax was a charming, dazzling, tantalizing female who lived nearby and who he felt was special. Her father, Lord Thomas Fairfax, and her husband, George William Fairfax, befriended George Washington in many ways. His first employment was as a surveyor for them; his principal travelling companions at that time were the Fairfaxes. In large measure, George William Fairfax was also a replacement for Washington's father, who had died about five years earlier, when George was a boy of only eleven years. And this good man's wife, Sally, was such a fascinating person. Womanhood at its fullest and finest, in the eyes of romantic sixteen-year-old George Washington.

Sally Fairfax was born in 1730, married on December 12, 1748, at age eighteen, and died in England at the age of eighty-one. She had a long face with a sharp chin. Her high forehead was surrounded by dark brown hair. Dark eyebrows arched over her large, brown, deeply set eyes. Her nose was classic, blending perfectly with the entire line of her forehead and face. She had a long, shapely, feminine neck set on moderately sloping soft shoulders. An attractive woman, but not a raving beauty.

Her principal attraction to George Washington was not in her physical appearance, although some writers have suggested he was definitely sexually attracted to her. Her main attraction to him was in her elusive mannerisms, her teasing ways, her coquettishness, her good humor. These personality traits were also what frustrated and perplexed him so much. At the same time he was intrigued by her playfulness, her imagination, and her bewitching qualities, he was also stymied by her evasiveness, her giddiness, and her intermittent flattery. To George, Sally was like a water faucet—hot and cold. Her communications with him were coy, saucy, teasing; then quickly they would switch to evasive, cold, distant, indifferent.

At least during the first ten years they knew each other, Sally

Fairfax and George Washington acted as if they were combatants on an emotional battlefield. He would advance the suggestion in 1755 that she write to him. She would counter by telling him to communicate with her only through a friend, not to write directly to her. She did not write to him at all for three long years, 1755 to 1758. They did, however, continue to be good friends. George Washington entertained Sally and her husband, for example, at Williamsburg in the spring of 1757. Because Sally would not write to him, George would withdraw at this point, only to find Sally taking up the initiative by sending word to him in a saucy, impertinent, barbing manner to the effect that he does not come often enough to her home and tell her of his travels and adventures. George would then again take the initiative, feeling encouragement, only to find Sally acting quite reserved, quite indifferent about what he was doing with himself. Back to discouragement.

But when Washington became very ill in 1758, Sally Fairfax cooked up some of her own recipes of jellies, teas, and similar nourishment. She expressed concern for his health and went out of her way to help him recuperate fully and quickly. She prepared, and personally delivered, those items she thought would help make him well so that he would be his usual self again. It was more than a kind act by a good neighbor; it had the loving hand of a woman who seemed to care in a special way.

The battle continued. George Washington and Martha Dandridge Custis had been engaged for almost six months, and George was miles away fighting in the Indian wars. The couple planned to be wed as soon as George returned from the wars. Sally Fairfax grabbed at this schedule. She fired off a shot; she kiddingly let him know she thought he was impatient to end the wars solely owing to his eagerness to marry Martha. George was hit by this barb and fired off a lengthy letter to Sally, dated September 12, 1758. In it he said he was doing his military job properly and with noble intentions. He believed in the cause and in the manner in which it was being conducted. "You destroy the merit of it entirely by attributing my anxiety to the prospect of possessing Mrs. Custis," George protestingly wrote. And then George Washington let all his

19

emotional guards and barriers down; his letter confessed openly, directly, and assuredly, his love for Sally. He told her then what he had been thinking, with ever-increasing passion, for the past ten years. He wrote:

> . . . you have drawn me, or rather I have drawn myself, into an honest confession of a simple fact. Misconstrue not my meaning, doubt it not, nor expose it. The world has no business to know the object of my Love, declared in this manner to you, when I want to conceal it. I do believe you are as happy as you say. Mirth, good humor, ease of mind—what else?—cannot fail to render you so and consummate your wishes.

"One thing above all things in this world I wish to know," he wrote —did Sally love him too?

Sally replied promptly, on September 23 or 24. But she avoided George's confession of love—she wrote a chatty letter about local social events and added that she knew he would be happy with Martha. She wrote nothing at all to answer George's plea for an expression of her feelings for him. She ignored that aspect, as well as his confession of his love for her. She had retreated fully at this attempt by him to join the emotional battle in earnest.

George was shocked and stunned. He did not anticipate this rejection. So he immediately took the aggressor's role again. On September 25, 1758, he blasted out: "Do we still misunderstand the true meaning of each other's letters?" And then once again Washington let the emotional guards and barriers down. "I cannot speak plainer," he wrote. Instintively, however, he immediately put some protection back into place. "But I'll say no more and leave you to guess the rest." Sally did not come out into the open; she did not accept the challenge; she did not reply to this second attempt by him to do battle in the open, with total directness, on their emotional battlefield. Instead, she withdrew, probably realizing that she could not continue this struggle without exposing her own innermost feelings for him, or without severely, perhaps permanently, damaging her combatant. Such stakes were too high. Sally Fairfax was not prepared to take such risks. And so George

Washington realized that the battle would never be joined. He did not again make an all-out effort until almost forty years later.

It is important to note that Sally Fairfax retained, throughout all the years, George Washington's letters to her. This suggests strongly that her own interest, her own attitude, her own feelings for him were somewhat affectionate, at the least. She must have appreciated this young man's attention, and she most likely derived considerable personal contentment from knowing George's feelings for her, especially as life went along and he rose to greater and greater fame.

The emotional battle with Sally Fairfax ended soon before George Washington married Martha Dandridge Custis on January 6, 1759. But their relationship continued; it was friendly, free, and open. The two potential combatants never met in a full, fierce conflict and therefore each was left with the ability and desire to continue to share visits and communicate with each other. Sally visited at George's home at Mount Vernon several times. And George visited at her home at least thirty-seven times between the days of those climatic letters in 1758 and the time she and her husband sailed for England in 1773, never to set foot in this country again.

George Washington's diary has two pertinent entries:

July 8, 1773: ". . . Colo. Fairfax and Mrs. Fairfax came in aftern. to take leave of us. . . ."

July 9, 1773: ". . . Mrs. Washington and self went to Belvoir to see them take Shipping. . . ."

More than one writer over the years has tried to put into words George Washington's thoughts and feelings as he watched his love for the past twenty-five years prepare to leave on the trip to her new home, her new life, in England. He now had to face reality in a private way, and to an extent greater than he had ever had to do before. At age forty-one, some writers say, Washington's most personal and emotional private life collapsed; Sally Fairfax was gone.

Sally Fairfax had been a lively and good-humored companion for George Washington. He said she had "mirth, good humor, ease of mind." In her youth, Sally was giddy, fun, a flirt to George. By middle age, she showed a more serious vein. She was then said to be a lady with a strong mind and exceptionally high principles.

But there had to be a big element of reserve involved on both sides in this total affair. Sally was, during the entire time, a married woman, and apparently contentedly so. George was floundering romantically for the first ten years. Then he settled into a satisfactory marriage with a good woman, "a quiet wife, a quiet soul." Martha Washington was no flirt; Sally Fairfax was. Martha did not baffle and confuse George; Sally did. Martha did not see George get carried away with his emotions; Sally did see this on more than one occasion. Martha did comfort George and let him live serenely; Sally delighted in throwing him off-balance by showing alternating and uncertain, unclear emotions toward him. Martha was good for George and most understanding and helpful about his military and public service; we are not at all sure that Sally would have been. Sally taught George to curb his strongest passions, his fullest emotions, his deepest feelings; Martha did not have to do this, for she rarely saw George display any of them toward her. George himself was to confide in Eliza Powel that love letters from Martha to him were more full of "friendship" than of "enamored love"; "to give the sheets warmth, one would have to set them on fire."

Jealousy? At first glance the Sally/George relationship might have been expected to contain some measure of this element—but it did not. If anything, Sally's husband and George became even closer personal friends because they both knew and cared for the same woman. Several writers have said that George William Fairfax never seemed in the slightest degree anything but pleased that George was fond of Sally. It has been suggested that he relished and made light of some of George's frustrations—after all, Mr. Fairfax *had* the prize. Mr. Washington's attempts were in vain right from the start.

And as the years went on and the four people involved became closer and closer friends, there was no real evidence of jealousy. Martha Washington could not help but know of George's feelings for Sally. But she also knew it could not materialize into anything destructive to her own relationship with George. Martha had known a serene and happy first love and marriage to Mr. Custis; her second venture was a practical, realistic marriage of convenience. She did not expect young, passionate love from George and she did not get it. What she did get was of more lasting value, forty years of marriage that brought full and truly meaningful love. A shared life. And so, conclude most writers, Martha Washington could and easily did accept George's emotional thoughts about Sally Fairfax. She had no important reason to be jealous and she simply was not.

Whatever the relationship of George and Sally was before Martha entered the scene, it then became a completely acceptable friendship in which Martha herself got as much satisfaction and pleasure as any of the other three participants.

The years rolled by from the time Sally Fairfax left Virginia in 1773, and it was then May of 1798. George Washington was back at his beloved Mount Vernon estate, finished with both his revolutionary army and his presidential service. He was, by then, a tired, old, senior warrior of the military and political battles. He would be dead in approximately a year-and-a-half.

The old man must have been reflecting on his own life. He took up the pen and wrote to his dear old neighbor and friend, Sally Fairfax, in England. His letter of May 16, 1798, began in the mood he was then in. He noted that twenty-five years had passed and that during this period "so many important events have occurred and such changes in man and things have taken place."

Once again George Washington entered the emotional battlefield with Sally Fairfax. His letter said, "None of which events however nor all of them together have been able to eradicate from my mind the recollection of those happy moments, the happiest of my life which I have enjoyed in your company."

And then the old warrior, who had seen so much death and destruction and ruin during the war, reflected on the ruins at Belvoir (the house had burned to the ground) and wrote further: ". . . when I cast my eyes towards Belvoir, which I often do to reflect the former Inhabitants of it, with whom we lived in such harmony and friendship . . . the ruins can only be viewed as momentos of former pleasures. . . ."

The old combatant then again drew his sword and made another attempt to resume the battle he and Sally Fairfax had last considered in 1758, forty years earlier. George Washington wrote, ". . . I have wondered often (your nearest relatives being in this country) that you should not prefer spending the Evening of your life among them rather than close the scene in a foreign country. . . . "

Come back, Sally; come back, Sally, he was saying. This time, of course, he was older, much less direct and less positive about exposing his feelings than he had been in 1758. He made it appear on the surface, at least, that Sally Fairfax would enjoy being with her relatives. He never said in so many words, that he, George Washington, wanted so much to see her again and wished that they might share their late life nearer each other. And this time he did not directly place any obligation on Sally to re-examine her feelings toward him. The attempt to draw her out onto their emotional battlefield was not aggressive; it was not a strong challenge. He definitely opened the possibility but did not push and force it the way he had forty years earlier. He had learned Sally's best teaching well—curb the emotions, retrain the passions, accept the facts and the reality of the situation.

Whatever her inner reactions were to George's attempt to see her again in the twilight of life, she did not express them. She withdrew fully, just as she had done in 1758.

Sally Fairfax is not known to have replied to George Washington's last letter to her. She never returned to the United States. She died in England in 1811, having lived there for the final thirty-eight years of her life.

Sally Fairfax had been a strong, lifelong influence on George Washington. A secret love for ten years; then an expressed love; then an unashamed, open, continuous friend for fifteen years; then twenty-five years of silent, private thoughts; and then an old man's final effort to regain his precious, personal, youthful love; to rekindle his greatest and most significant personal feelings and experiences.

Through all this, Sally preserved George's letters to her. Is it too farfetched to visualize an old woman sitting quietly, basking in, and reflecting fondly on, her own part in such an amazing relationship? Was the earlier coyness and evasiveness real, or was it a facade put up by a potentially vulnerable woman who simply had to withdraw and stay away from a showdown of emotions with this persistent admirer?

Sally Fairfax never had any children of her own. George Washington never had any children of his own.

Whether the exact nature of their relationship can or cannot ever be defined adequately and definitively and authoritatively, it seems, to this writer at least, sufficiently clear that Sally Fairfax was the most significant love in George Washington's life. The indications are overwhelmingly persuasive that this woman, more than any other he knew, moved George Washington into real, responsible, manhood. Sally Fairfax left a clear, distinct, certain mark on George Washington's character and on his capacity to become the highly revered man he was then and still is today.

Sally Fairfax, more than any other woman, was the true love of his life. She was the most pleasant memory of an old man's entire lifetime. And she was the one who repeatedly refused to do full and total emotional battle with him. It is hard to believe that Sally Fairfax did not love George Washington, probably in a better way than he ever realized—surely in a different way than he pleaded for. Most likely she loved him in a way that was the only possible acceptable way for her.

Sally Fairfax could be the effective teacher to him of a total sense of reality. The teacher herself possessed it to a huge degree.

6

Martha Dandridge Custis Washington

Martha Dandridge Custis and George Washington were married on January 6, 1759 in an early afternoon ceremony performed by the Reverend David Mossom, rector of St. Peter's Church (Episcopal). The nuptials took place at the bride's home, White House Plantation, New Kent County, Virginia. A reception followed immediately.

THAT ANNOUNCEMENT sums up the basic facts for these two individuals who would share more than forty years of life as husband and wife.

On their wedding day, Martha Custis was age twenty-seven-and-a-half and George would be twenty-seven about six weeks later. It was his first marriage; Martha had been married once before.

Her first husband, Daniel Parke Custis, died on July 8, 1757, at age forty-five years, nine months. They had been married eight years and had four children. The first- and second-born (Daniel Parke Custis and Frances Custis) died in infancy. John Parke Custis (Jackie) and Martha Parke Custis (Patsy) survived. Jackie was aged four and Patsy aged two when their mother married George Washington. Tragically, both had short lives—hers ended at age eighteen, his at age twenty-seven. As it developed, Jackie and Patsy were the only children George and Martha Washington were to have. No children were born to them during their forty years of marriage.

Most biographers say that it is probable that George Washington had met Martha Custis at various social events before she was widowed. The two were known to have attended some of the same dances and parties, and it is a reasonable assumption they would have been introduced. However, no substantial proof has come to light to satisfy biographers that they did actually meet until approximately eight months after her husband died.

George and Martha were together on March 16, 1758. Whether they had been introduced before that date or not, this meeting was the first at which they spent any significant amount of time in each other's company, particularly as two "eligible" individuals. Martha was a guest at the home of her neighbor, William Chamberlayne, and George was enroute to Williamsburg. When his boat docked in New Kent, Mr. Chamberlayne invited George to dinner. He accepted, was formally introduced to Martha, and apparently was seated next to her at the table.

The mutual interest and attraction was immediate. George canceled his plans to continue on to Williamsburg that same day. This caused some disruption to those traveling with George, and was a highly irregular thing for him to do. He stayed overnight at Chamberlayne's and on into the late afternoon the following day.

A few days later, on March 25, George called upon Martha at her own home. This required a courtship trip of thirty-three miles on horseback from Williamsburg. Virtually all biographers say that George Washington proposed marriage to Martha Custis on March 25, at her home. And even the most cautious and careful writers conclude that either (a) Martha accepted the proposal on that same day, or (b) she gave George definite assurance that she would give his proposal prompt consideration.

It is a virtual certainty that each knew a great deal about the other by reputation in this small geographical area and by being in the same social circles. George had built a fine reputation as a colonel in the Indian wars, as a leader in Virginia politics, as a substantial farmer in Fairfax County, and as a most eligible bachelor in the social life of Williamsburg. Martha was generally considered one of the nicest and wealthiest widows in Virginia and a popular, much-sought-after guest and companion in Williamsburg society.

Most observers assert that it was a mutually prudent and sensible engagement. It would be a *marriage of convenience.* Martha would bring into it an inherited fortune (over 17,400 acres of real estate plus £23,632—$600,000–800,000 in today's money—in cash, slaves, livestock, crops, and securities); two young children; her own personal beauty, grace, and charm; and proven talent to run the household of a large plantation. (Martha had been executrix of her husband's estate and showed considerable ability in handling all the details.) George would bring into it skills as a business and financial manager; as a guardian for the two children; and as an attractive man. She would be a warm personal companion and an ideal hostess, a definite asset in his budding career. He would be an ideal new father for her children and a strong protector of her wealth.

The potential for such a gifted and talented couple was awesome to consider.

However, it was not a love match. Both knew the other was not the first or greatest love. George Washington's earlier affection for Sally Fairfax continued in strong evidence all his life. Martha, having had the security of a happy prior marriage (her marriage to Custis has been called a "match of deep affection"), seemed to understand and not be overly upset by George's feelings for Sally Fairfax. Martha also knew that Sally was contentedly married to someone else from the time George became infatuated with Sally, when he was age sixteen until very late in his life. Martha had plenty of practical common sense.

The couple promptly set about making preparations for a wedding. In April, 1758, less than two weeks after the engagement, Martha Custis wrote to her clothier in London for ". . . one genteel suite of clothes for myself to be grave but not to be extravagent and not to be mourning . . ." She also ordered enough yellow brocaded grosgrain silk to make a costume, some pink lukestring, a white and garnet egret and a long white necklace. Martha's letter included an intimate item: ". . . I have sent a night gound to be dide of a fashionable coler fitt for me to ware . . ."

On May 4, 1758, about five weeks after the engagement, George ordered a wedding ring from Philadelphia; it cost the then considerable sum of £2,16 shillings.

Few reliable facts have been found about the personal relationship during the engagement period. George was miles away fighting in the Indian wars for those eight months. The relationship would have to be by letters. But, to the eternal frustration of historians, Martha burned virtually all her letters from George shortly after his death in 1799. Included in the destruction were any premarriage letters, in addition to the accumulation during forty years of marriage. Only one letter appears, and it is referred to by many writers as the "first love letter" from George to Martha. It reads in full as follows:

> July 20, 1758
>
> We have begun our march for the Ohio. A courier is starting for Williamsburg and I embrace the opportunity to send a few words to one whose life is now inseparable from mine. Since that happy hour when we made our pledges to each other, my thoughts have been continually going to you as to another Self. That an all-powerful Providence may keep us both in safety is the prayer of your ever faithful and affectionate friend.

Romanticists like this letter, but there is considerable doubt that it was actually written by George Washington. One of Washington's most respected biographers, Douglas Southall Freeman, concludes it is a forgery. In making a scholarly and astute detailed analysis, Freeman's main reasons for deciding it is a forgery are: (1) it is worded and written in a style and contains spelling that simply cannot be George Washington's and (2) factually no such march was planned on or about the indicated date.

The wedding day, January 6, 1759, began with light snow flurries on the hard-frozen ground. Martha's home, White House Plantation, on the banks of the Pamunkey River, New Kent County,

Virginia, burst into frenzied activity. The outdoor kitchen and smoke house were in operation. Inside, the floors were being polished, fires started in each fireplace, fresh white candles put into sconces and chandeliers. Large platters of ham and chicken were prepared. Cakes were set up. Wine and rum were carried up from the cellar.

George Washington arrived on the scene from Williamsburg on horseback, in the early morning. It was to be a wedding ceremony attended by Virginia aristocracy, friends, and neighbors. Guests began to arrive about noon and were helped from coaches and carriages by servants dressed in white and purple livery. The frozen ground became muddy from the carriage wheels. Among the guests were the Governor of Virginia, Francis Fauquier, wearing scarlet and gold, and the Speaker of the House of Burgesses, John Robinson.

The ceremony was performed about 1:30 or 2:00 P.M. The exact hour seems impossible to determine. Governor Fauquier was among the last to arrive, and it appears that he came after 1:00 P.M. The bride was clad in yellow brocaded grosgrain silk, trimmed with pink lukestring, and was bedecked with matching earrings, bracelet, and necklace of white pearls. She wore diamond buckles on her tiny, white satin slippers. The bridegroom wore his new Virginia Regiment uniform of blue cloth lined with red silk over an embroidered white satin waistcoat, with white gloves, gold shoebuckles, and a straight dress sword.

Martha Custis stood five feet tall; George Washington was six feet two inches. Martha was plump, with small hands and feet. George was slender and muscular with huge hands and size thirteen shoes. Martha's dark hair set off her hazel eyes, wide brows, strongly curved nose, and soft, round chin. George's hair was auburn, and he had blue grey eyes; his features were sharp and well defined. A striking couple—she so petite, diminutive, feminine; he so tall, large-boned, athletic, masculine.

George's affectionate and pet nickname for Martha was "Patsy." Martha privately called George her "old man."

The couple joined hands in the drawing room before the

Reverend Mr. Mossom. They stood beneath a chandelier holding four white candles. At least six sconces, each with two white candles, were in the room. The best evidence is that thirty-six to forty guests attended the ceremony, with about a dozen servants peeking into the room, as the two became man and wife.

In accord with the custom of the times, the bride and groom did not go off on a honeymoon but stayed and entertained their most intimate friends. "Feasting and festivity continued unabated for about three full days. Biographers have called it a "tireless orgy of festivities." George is reported to have danced with every woman at least once. Martha, a bit more shy and modest, and decidedly less vigorous, apparently was less accommodating to each and every male guest.

When the celebration finally ended, George and Martha Washington continued to live at her home. He journeyed to Williamsburg so he could attend to his political duties as an elected member of the House of Burgesses, which duties began on his twenty-seventh birthday, February 22, 1759.

The couple were also waiting for George's home at Mount Vernon to be readied. George, during the engagement period, had ordered the addition of one story to the original one-and-a-half-story house in preparation for his new wife and her two children. And shortly before leaving White House Plantation, he instructed his overseer at Mount Vernon to have the "house very well cleanned" and "you must get two of the best Bedspreads put up" and "get some eggs and chickens, and prepare in the best manner you can."

They arrived with full bag and baggage—trunkloads of personal belongings and their worldly possessions—exactly three months after their wedding day, that is, on April 6, 1759. The couple would consider Mount Vernon their marital home for the next forty years.

During their forty years of marriage, several aspects of Martha Washington's personality and mannerisms are in constant evidence.

First, Martha Washington insisted on being "fashionable." She wore plain clothes made of the finest and latest materials. She also usually wore a headdress; she preferred to be seen with a cap on, and frequently the cap was showy and elaborate. Not an elegant dresser, Martha showed quiet good taste in her dress. She was "scrupulously neat."

Second, Martha Washington was unassuming. She willingly took the role of companion to, but never competitor with, her husband. She was there. She was pleasant, polite, quiet. A gracious, dignified, respectful hostess. One writer says that from the time she was married in 1759 until George became first president of the United States in 1789, virtually no one paid much attention to Martha Washington. She was there, always there, but stayed totally in the background. And after she became first lady of the land, she continued to prefer a largely inactive role. But now her high position drew more attention to her as a separate personality.

Third, Martha Washington was unfailingly discreet. She never spoke out of turn. She never discussed anything that George was planning or thinking. In addition to their private conversations as husband and wife, Martha sat in on many serious discussions of military strategy and governmental policy. She did not participate, offered no viewpoints; she simply was there and heard it all. Under the circumstances, the opportunity was great for a woman to talk about what was being planned, to brag a little about her husband's role in it all. Martha did not do that. She had total discretion and kept her mouth shut, tightly shut. Martha's discretion was invaluable to George. His friends could speak freely and openly. This was a tremendous asset to him in all his relationships during the war and in the presidency.

Fourth, Martha Washington was the perfect hostess. Author James Thomas Flexner says that between 1768 and 1775 the Washingtons entertained "about 2,000 guests." Martha took to the duties with relish. She considered an empty house a dull house. Martha was an extremely early riser, up every day well before daybreak and immediately active in household management. She was remarkably efficient at it. She planned, supervised, and controlled the entire show. Her discipline to servants was both humane and prompt. The Washington household, whether at Mount Vernon or elsewhere, was bustling. Expected and unexpected guests and visitors, neighbors, and sightseers, came and went day after day. Often they shared a meal, sometimes breakfast, sometimes dinner, sometimes only tea and cakes, with George and Martha Washington. It was such an active scene that George Washington wrote in 1797: "Unless someone pops in unexpectedly, Mrs. Washington and myself will do what I believe has not been done within the last 20 years by us, that is to set down to dinner by ourselves."

Fifth, Martha Washington was a deeply religious person. Her grandson remembered that "every day of her adult life," after breakfast, she would retire to her bedroom and meditate, pray, and read the Holy Scriptures for about one hour. She and George often attended church services together, and he served as vestryman of their parish. But it was Martha who was the religious backbone of the family. In keeping with her unassuming manner generally, she did not flaunt her religious beliefs. She kept them within herself, as a quiet, personal attitude and strength.

Sixth, Martha Washington was a family person. She loved her family, her home life, her simple pleasures with children. Her daughter, Patsy, died at age seventeen. Her granddaughter, Nelly, then lived with Martha and George from age two to age twenty. And Martha doted on all four of her son's children. She treated the black servant girl, Oney Judge, almost as her own child, and sat with her and sewed by the hour, day after day. Babies, young children, budding teenagers—all had Martha's full, caring attention.

Seventh, Martha Washington was George Washington's best friend. She gave him what he craved most and enjoyed most, what sustained him throughout his long and varied military and political career—a happy home. For forty years, Martha gave George the comfort, serenity, and peacefulness he longed for. She provided him with "domestic enjoyments" to the fullest extent. She came to love Mount Vernon and her life-style there fully. She spoke of her days in New York and Philadelphia as "lost days." Mount Vernon was the comfortable place to her. There she called herself "an old-fashioned housekeeper, steady as a clock, busy as a bee, and cheerful as a cricket." Martha Washington's cheerfulness soothed George's anxieties. She softened his difficult hours. Her firmness inspired confidence. Her devotional piety instilled a hopeful and optimistic outlook even in his darkest hours during the war. Martha was pleasant company for George Washington.

Eighth. Not witty, nor particularly brilliant, nor articulate, nor imaginative, Martha Washington's best talents and effectiveness ran to relationships with people. She had an ease, an elegance, a pleasantness, a cheerfulness, a dignity, a gentle nature, and an unerring instinct for getting along with people, all people. She loved them and they reciprocated. Martha appeared to be happiest and most content, whenever she was near her husband, her "old man." Regardless of what was going on, regardless of who else was there, Martha delighted in being near her husband.

At age forty-four, Martha Washington was described as being tiny, shy, and fat. She then ordered gloves "to fit a small hand and a pretty large arm." Not a strikingly pretty woman, she was handsome and unpretentiously attractive. She had clear hazel eyes, a large hooked nose, a small mouth and a well-rounded chin. Her clothing was plain and muted in color. Martha was "well-groomed" but not overdressed: a true gentlewoman. She was once described by a visitor at Valley Forge as similar to a "Roman matron of whom I had read so much." By age fifty-eight, Martha Washington was described as "a trifle dowdy, naive, grandmotherly." Her hair was then white, her teeth "beautiful."

The Revolutionary War period was particularly difficult for Martha Washington. Her husband was away from home for over eight years. Her son was killed at age twenty-seven, fighting at Yorktown. When George Washington first became General of the Armies he wrote to Martha and promised "I shall return safe to you." He thought he would return by the next fall, a few months later. It was eight years later that he returned to Martha at Mount Vernon. In breaking the news of his selection as general, George minimized the physical risks involved to himself, and he ignored his own personal inconveniences. He wrote, ". . . my unhappiness will flow from the uneasiness I know you will feel from being left alone." George assured Martha "I retain an unalterable affection for you which neither time or distance can change." George wore a miniature portrait of Martha around his neck for the last twenty-four years of his life. It had been made at his request by Charles Wilson Peale.

A regular pattern for Martha Washington developed during the war years. On her shoulders fell the job of managing Mount Vernon and George's personal affairs. But she left Mount Vernon every year to be with George when there was no fighting. As soon as the first shot was fired, however, Martha headed back to Mount Vernon. Writers from the past say: "Mrs. Washington, according to her custom, marched home when the campaign was about to open." Martha said she had to be with her husband whenever possible because "the poor General was so unhappy that it distresses me greatly." She first went north to Cambridge, Massachusetts, in December, 1775; thereafter, she regularly went to wherever her husband had set up his headquarters.

Martha detested the war, the bloodshed, the human suffering. She herself said: "I shudder every time I hear the sound of a gun."

All during the war, Martha Washington was referred to as "Lady Washington." She and the General greeted officers, troops, visitors, and local inhabitants with benevolence and gentleness. Martha personally nursed a young Spanish soldier who was ill with pneunomia, but to no avail; he died within three days. At Valley Forge she vicariously suffered with the troops in their small, cold huts. At Morristown, Martha was scared at having to sleep with the windows tightly shuttered, guards constantly on duty, her privacy nil. At Newburgh, New York, Martha continued her long and arduous duties as mistress of the General's headquarters. It is interesting to note that George Washington charged Congress for Martha's expenses in coming to his military headquarters throughout the war. He did so because he himself did not take a leave of absence as the other officers periodically did; instead, George Washington brought his "home" to wherever he was.

The relief was tremendous when finally on Christmas Eve, 1783, George Washington rode up to Mount Vernon and found wife

Martha standing at the doorway to greet him. She thought she was welcoming him home permanently.

The "permanence" was short-lived. About five years later, George became president of the United States. Martha delayed in joining him in this new and demanding public service. But join him she did and took up her new duties as first lady. Her hair was now set and dressed every day. Her clothing and social obligations left little time for personal pleasures, little time for grandma to dote over and enjoy her grandchildren. As first lady, Martha never participated in the discussions of serious governmental afffairs. She listened, played the role of hostess to the highest levels of officials and their ladies, and earned the respect and veneration of all who crossed her path in those eight years of presidential life. Martha was the "unassuming lady who creates love and esteem." A perfect part of the new government. A kind person. "Not the tincture of hauteur about her," said Mrs. John Adams.

During the presidential years, Martha Washington regularly met the ladies in her drawing room. Every Friday night from seven o'clock to ten o'clock women could call on and chat with the first lady.

Martha Washington rarely showed emotion in public. She was calmly dignified most of the time. One exception occurred at the last ball she attended as wife of the president. Thousands of guests poured out to be with the Washingtons on February 22, 1797, and "Martha Washington was moved to tears," at this overwhelming display of respect and affection for them. Martha was basically a humble person. She could say after a reception: "I left in as great pomp as if I had been some great body."

In the last year or two before George died, Martha was not lively company for him. She had grown exhausted at the years of constant social demands, the constant stream of guests. Household management became a chore. Company became a bother. Martha fatigued easily. The strain of years of doing her duty as wife to this busy, prominent man showed all too much. Martha Washington was simply ready to unwind herself and relax.

After George died on December 14, 1799, Martha became sad

and lonely. She let the Mount Vernon estate fall into a run-down condition. She could no longer support and manage the three hundred slaves. She could no longer handle the household and the plantation. Mrs. John Adams visited her a year after George had died. She was saddened by what she saw in both the property and the person of Martha Washington. She reported that "Mrs. Washington's spirit in life was gone."

Martha Washington died at Mount Vernon on May 22, 1802. Cause of death was bilious fever and complications. She was then aged seventy-one. Her body was put to eternal rest next to her husband's in the family vault. She was eulogized as a lady who had "dignity of manners, superiority of human understanding, a mind intelligent and elevated." And just as her husband's memory has been honored through the years, so has hers been honored. Martha's picture is used on commemorative coins and medals, plates, plaques, postage stamps, on bric-a-brac of every kind and description.

George Washington rarely spoke of Martha Washington with deeply affectionate words. The word *love,* for example, was almost never used. His last will and testament comes closest; in it he referred to her as "my dearly beloved wife Martha." In referring to a batch of love letters that Mrs. Eliza Powel found in a personal desk given to her by George Washington at the end of his presidency, George said the letters from Martha to him were filled more with "friendship than enamoured love. A reader of the 'romantic order' could only have given the sheets warmth by setting them on fire."

To the eternal frustration of historians and biographers, Martha Washington burned virtually all her letters from George soon after his death. If there were words of deep affection, of love, in such letters, they are forever blocked from view by the public. The best evidence available suggests that few, if any, romantic, loving phrases would have appeared. Martha was the best female friend, true friend George ever had. This woman was what he needed during his life. She gave him a balanced, happy, private home life to offset his hectic, trying public life. She understood George's talents, his real needs, his personality. George Washington found her to be "a quiet wife, a quiet soul; an agreeable consort for life."

Many observers on the scene, as well as later ones, have considered George and Martha the perfect couple who meshed so well and complimented each other ideally. Vice President John Adams summed it up, and paid perhaps the highest possible tribute to Martha Washington when he questioned: "Would Washington have been the Commander of the Revolutionary Army or the President of the United States if he had not married this rich widow?"

7

Mary Ball Washington

MARY BALL WASHINGTON was George Washington's mother. As his mother, she had a greater influence than many of the other women in his life. The nature of that influence and the extent of their relationship are examined here.

This relationship of mother and son is best summed up in the words of the foremost biographer of Washington, Douglas Southall Freeman. He said it was a "strange mystery." George Washington did not love his mother and most observers have concluded that he did not even like her. That is the strange mystery—George's lack of affection for his mother; his lifelong avoidance of her; his willingness to do his filial duty but very little more. And for her part, she showed no natural motherly joy in his accomplishments, did not take part in his moments of glory, did not exert herself to express or demonstrate to her son that she was proud of him. Their relationship was one of blood—not of friendship, not of love and mutual caring, not of affection and mutual respect.

Mary Ball Washington was born in the winter of 1708. She was twenty-three when she married Augustine Washington on March 6, 1731. Her husband was then a widower with three children. It was her first marriage, and by the standards in those times, Mary Ball was considered a spinster whose physical plumpness and domineering personality had been drawbacks to her attractiveness as a marriageable woman.

Their first child was George Washington, born on February 22,

1732. Augustine died when George was only a boy of eleven years, and his mother shouldered the responsibility of raising him to manhood. This situation and burden might have produced sympathetic understanding and a close tie between mother and son. In fact, it produced the opposite.

At this point, some readers may question this harsh judgment, this sad conclusion. They may think it is only one writer's interpretation. That same conclusion, however, is reached by virtually all of Washington's biographers. Here is the way some others have summarized the lifelong relationship of Mary Ball Washington and George Washinton:

Douglas Southall Freeman——The strangest mystery of Washington's life is his lack of affection for his mother. Added years brought no improvement in his relations with her.

James Thomas Flexner——This relationship was always stormy.

North Callahan——Washington and his mother did not get along very well.

Woodrow Wilson——She had never been tender to her son.

Richard M. Ketchum——George Washington found his mother a powerful, strong-willed, demanding and extremely difficult parent.

Burke Davis——The querulous, penurious Mary Ball Washington had long been resentful of George's attention to affairs other than her own.

Ralph K. Andrist——Mary Ball Washington made excessive demands on her children, and later evidenced not the slightest pride in her illustrious son's accomplishments.

Shelby Little——Washington never loved the domineering and embarrassing old lady very tenderly, but he had, within limits, always been dutiful.

May Ball Washington lived at Ferry Farm until September, 1771. George then set her up in a small, elegant house in Fredericksburg, Virginia. He visited her in Fredericksburg a few times between 1772 and 1789, the year of her death. His personal diary shows these kinds of entries:

September 14, 1772——"Lodgd at my Mother's"

December 8, 1773——"Breafasted with my Mother." George gave her £30 cash.

May 5, 1775——"Spent half an hour with my Mother." George was in Fredericksburg on several other days, but there is no record that he stopped to see her at all. He often stayed overnight in Fredericksburg, and his diary names the place where he slept; it rarely was his mother's home.

Mary Ball Washington was a grasping, vulgar, argumentative person. She was a strict, domineering individual. Some writers have summed her up as a total shrew. She raised her baby son with undue concern for his health, his whereabouts, his habits. She showed repeated displays of exaggerated anxiety over him and frequently objected to any activity which might endanger him. She was possessive, too much so, about young George Washington.

The first major show of this concern occurred when George wanted, at his stepbrother's urging, to join the Royal Navy and go to sea at age fourteen as a midshipman. Family friends and neighbors encouraged George to seek this adventure, believing it would help him grow and mature in the male-oriented world of 1746. Without a father at home, George could use the masculine contacts. His mother, however, objected and, in fact, absolutely refused to permit it. She asserted all her influence as his mother and protector and overruled the others. George Washington did not go to sea.

The mother's influence, as later events developed, was fortunate. Her pleas that he stay home rather than join the British fleet proved beneficial to all concerned. At the time it was made, however, the decision was a difficult first test of George's wishes pitted against his mother's powerfully strong will.

A second conflict arouse when George announced his intention to join the military exploits of General Edward Braddock in Ohio. His mother again protested. But this time, George, at age twenty-three, made the decision and went. Mary Ball Washington's expression of concern for his well-being and her attempts to keep him from danger were overruled by George's desire for a military adventure. It was a test of the natural concern of a mother to keep her son safe and within the nest against the son's need to develop his own interests and his own life-style. George Washington, the young man, was feeling his own needs more strongly than he had at the time he wanted to join the navy. So this time he risked the consequences of his mother's displeasure with his decision.

Mary Ball Washington was a terror around young boys when George was growing up. A close boyhood friend said: "I was 10 times more afraid of Mrs. Washington than of my own parents." She was reported to be such an awesome, bad-tempered woman that she "kept her children quiet just by her presence." She was strict, stern, bossy, with a hot temper—a real shrew. She made no bones about her personality and its effects on other people, particularly younger ones. She did just as she pleased, and to hell with what others thought.

By the time George was twenty-five the relationship was strained, fully and materially, in all aspects. George would no longer live near his mother. He rarely discussed anything of importance with her. He went about his own affairs paying very little attention to what she said or suggested. He did look after her financial needs, made sure she had ample cash and other necessities of life, and was a dutiful son—but one who showed virtually no affection for the woman who bore him.

One of George Washington's greatest traits—self-reliance—came from his desire to escape a home where his dominant, demanding mother rules in such a way as to make him feel uncomfortable and discontented. He knew no genuinely happy home life as a boy, so he longed for that even more as a man. Frequently he would return to Mount Vernon for rest, relaxation, and serenity during the years of his strenuous military and political activities. Several writers say he longed for this more than most soldiers around him. His mother was not at Mount Vernon.

George Washington showed patience and deference to his mother as life went along, but he rarely wished to be with her and seldom shared any confidence with her. She was an embarrassment to him. An exceedingly frugal person, she carried this characteristic to ridiculous and crude extremes. A frequently written-about example is the occasion when she took a leg of mutton into her hands and sniffed it at the dinner table to make sure it was fit to eat, while at the same time sharply instructing servants and cooks in the sternest possible manner not to throw out any food regardless of its condition. The scene of a respected colonel of the Indian wars and an honored member of Virginia society having dinner with distinguished friends, when his mother uncouthly questions the quality of the meat in front of all, is a vivid picture of the strains on George's patience and feelings.

In money matters, Mary Ball Washington caused her son even more anguish. By all accounts, George gave her ample provisions and was generous in his support of her. His concern for her welfare was genuine and sincere, as well as thorough. Objective observers consistently declare that George did as much for his mother as was warranted by the facts, and many times far more. While he was miles away fighting in the war, she regularly informed him, practically nagged him, that she was starving and in dire need.

Two episodes regarding the financial relationship were so painful to George Washington that he got to the point where he would make note of the name of any person who was present when he gave his mother money. And he also made entries in his diary of the financial assistance he provided to her—again naming witnesses and setting down complete details.

The first episode happened in 1781 when Mary Ball Washington's constant complaining about her son's lack of concern for her led her to secretly petition the General Assembly of Virginia to award her a pension because she could not pay her property taxes. Mainly because George Washington was then serving in the army without pay, the General Assembly quickly passed an act doing so. George was extremely embarrassed, and as soon as word of this act reached him, he insisted on its repeal. Needless to say, he was furious and shocked by his mother's state of mind and her efforts to discredit him in the public's eye. The act was promptly repealed, and Mrs. Washington was left to her own assets, without public assistance. For a man of his wealth and position, the idea of his mother, in effect, on public welfare was too much to accept. The public pension certainly was not needed, whether or not George gave her any money. She had more than ample assets of her own, but they were being horribly mismanaged by her own weaknesses and by her stubbornness.

The second financial episode was in 1787, when she referred to George as a "delinquent and unjust and undutiful son." This description was made not just once but on a regular and continuing basis to all comers, to anyone who would lend an ear, everywhere she went. A worse maligner Washington rarely had. He exploded. Then he promptly set about, verbally and in writing, trying to get her affairs straightened out so there would be no question about her care. She had let the property get run-down and become badly neglected. Her closest neighbors considered her a poor overseer and manager of her affairs. So, George Washington urged her to rent out the farmland and use the income for her support. He urged her to reduce the number of servants and livestock so they would be less of a burden on her time and skills in the management of the property.

Mary Ball Washington rejected all these suggestions. Instead, she merely continued to declare that her son was thoughtless and uncaring and stingy. Her bitter and unfair comments continued to plague George Washington. George resented his mother's demands for money. She had ample resources of her own, and he already was giving her substantial additional amounts. One time he was told she was again broke, and he said: "She is upon all occasions and in all companies, complaining of her wants and difficulties." These complaints, he thought, "make her appear in an unfavorable view" and also put into an unfavorable light all "those who are connected with her." The embarrassment hurt George deeply. Any *real distress* to her would be helped; but this insignificant, unjustified, constant nagging and complaining would be ignored by him, as much as humanly possible.

The breech in the mother-son relationship was so complete by the year 1787 that in all his suggestions to her, George never invited her to live with him or under his roof under any circumstances. He told her that to live with him at Mount Vernon "will never answer your purposes in any shape whatsoever." He indicated that either (a) she

44

would be uncomfortable in the bustling entertainment scene he and his wife, Martha, knew at Mount Vernon, or (b) she would be essentially confined to her room and would be disturbed by the noise throughout the house. In either case, he was trying to let her know she would be unhappy. Obviously, he was also saying in loud, clear tones that she was not welcome. At first glance this might be seen as a somewhat selfish attitude for him to take. But, after thirty years of dickering, George made it abundantly plain that he was not anxious to put up with her vulgarity and rude behavior at a time in his life when the social aspects were essential to his reputation and position in the new nation, and indeed in the future demands for his public service. It seemed to be his strong viewpoint that the duty owed by a son to his mother in that period of time did not include upsetting his own comforts and life-style, particularly when she had a place of her own with ample servants and helpers and substantial resources available.

This writer has found no comments in any source mentioning the feelings of George's wife, Martha, for her mother-in-law. There is no indication that the two had any contacts with each other. No indication that Martha looked after Mary Ball Washington. No indication that Martha helped or tried to help George when his mother would haggard him with her complaints. No indication that their relationship was anything but a cold, indifferent one created by marriage but not by choice. These two women surely would have little in common, except for him. Martha, as a skilled, talented, and efficient manager of a large plantation household would have been disturbed by Mary's inadequacies in this area and in her refusals to be helped. Martha, as a gracious, dignified, and superb hostess, would surely have shared George's humiliations at Mary's vulgarity and lack of social graces. Thus, it would appear to be a reasonable conclusion that these two women in George Washington's life were so completely different in personality, temperament, and tastes that even the fact that they were related and had a common interest in the same man would not be enough. They just could not, and apparently did not, seek each other out and did not help each other in their daily lives.

Mary Ball Washington seemed to harbor a lifelong resentment of her son's successes and prestige. A few biographers have suggested this was a result of her own insecure mind, her deteriorating physical condition, and her basic inability to accept the fact that her boy had become a man. She developed, from 1758 on, a state of mind that fundamentally said others (and especially her son George) had to help her because she was unable to do for herself. She lacked confidence in her own talents and abilities to manage her own affairs. And she was so opinionated and strong willed that she rejected help from well-intentioned neighbors and friends.

Mary Ball Washington viewed her son's accomplishments with bitterness and resentment. Her comments came from her own selfish viewpoint. They reflected her attitude that whatever else he was doing was unimportant because it was at the expense of more attention to her. She accused him of "neglect." At the end of the French and Indian War, mother wrote about her son's activities, as follows: "No end to my trouble while George was in the Army." And later in life she was so openly scornful of his military career that many people said she was a Tory. The mother of the leader of the revolution did not accept and understand her son's views in the cause in which he was fighting. And around the time of her final suffering, just before she went speechless, fell into a coma and died, she still could not be tender and supportive. She told him his new duties as president of the United States would only prevent him from helping her now when she was in "great want."

Mary Ball Washington developed substantial breast cancer by 1787. This caused severe physical pain as well as deeper concern for her capacity to function. She expressed the need for even more care by her son. But by this time, after almost thirty years of unappreciated efforts, George was exasperated enough to merely try to make her into a quiet "fireside" figure.

Mary suffered breast cancer for almost two years. On August 10, 1789, she went speechless. On August 20 she lost consciousness and her condition became critical. About three o'clock in the afternoon on August 25, 1789, Mary Ball Washington was dead, in her own home in Fredericksburg. She was then eighty-one years old. She had suffered increasing physical pain. But she had maintained her stubborness right to the end: she refused to take the bottle of medicine prescribed for her. George reacted to the news of his mother's death with some emotion and even more philosophical resignation. He wrote that "awful and affecting as the death of a parent is" there is a "hope that she is translated into a happier place."

After a lifetime of storminess, indifference, and avoidance of each other, Mary Ball Washington showed she had not forgotten her son, George. Her last will left to him all her most personal belongings. She gave him the lion's share of her total assets. He was the principal beneficiary of her entire estate. George did not need this addition to his wealth as much as did several other relatives who were largely ignored in Mrs. Washington's last wishes. George was then president of the United States, a man of considerable wealth and position, far beyond other close relations of Mary Ball Washington. Yet, it was to her son, George, that mother showed generosity at death.

For many years, Mary Ball Washington never took part in any of her son's triumphs. She would not inconvenience herself and simply would not budge from her house to share his moments of glory. She did not attend when he was honored in Williamsburg, Virginia. She did not participate in any way when he became first president. She did not go out of her way in the slightest degree to show normal, motherly pride and admiration for him or his accomplishments at any stage of his career, whether military or political. She seemed to resent his activities and his prominence because she felt he would "neglect" her even more.

She ignored what was important and meaningful to him. In return, he virtually ignored her as a person for more than thirty years. George rarely invited his mother to participate in in any of his finer moments. His lifelong avoidance of her, conclude a few authors, was for valid, human reasons, and not as an arbitrary disdain for the woman who bore and raised him. She was fundamentally an unattractive human being, and the sole fact that she was his mother did not alter his reaction to this kind of person. It was not an unreasonable and snobbish approach; he had tried to help her, tried to show filial duty to her, but, in all candor, he did not like her, and he did not like her mannerisms as a person. By the time he became an adult, his mother simply was not "his kind" to associate with. It is said that people can chose their friends but not their relatives—George Washington just could not choose to have his mother for a friend too.

Between 1757 and 1787 George Washington apparently wrote no letters to his mother. Historians say that, of the six letters from him to her that survive, four were written in 1755, at the beginning of the time he was openly defying her and going his own way regardless of her wishes and pleas.

Illiterate, untidy, quarrelsome, she was a lifelong strain on her son. She was constantly demanding attention from him; constantly pleading for more care and more money from him. And for a Christmastime ball in Fredericksburg in 1783, mother sent word to George at the place where he was staying (also in Fredericksburg). She ordered him to come to her house and take her to that social event. George did so, reluctantly but dutifully. It has been written that with his seventy-four-year-old mother on his arm, George Washington entered the ballroom. Then he promptly left her and mingled with others for the balance of the evening.

Mary Ball Washington died on August 25, 1789, at age 81. Her son was beginning his first term as president. She had lived alone since her husband died forty-six years earlier. She had never remarried, had never begun a new life after Augustine Washington died in 1743. Her mental condition, probably not healthy even as a young woman, grew progressively worse as years went by. The most charitable comment about Mary's mind found in the books is that it was not "orderly." The final thirty-five or so years of her life seemed to be spent in self-pity, in selfish thoughts, in resentments over her son's progression as a major figure in the American Revolution and in the development of the new nation.

One is tempted to conclude that Mary Ball Washington's life was pathetic and unrewarding. So much failure and ineptitude shows up on her own part. And this sorrow was not even balanced by a natural joy and comfort from seeing her son amount to something worthwhile in their society and world. She seemed to fail to enjoy as much as a vicarious thrill at any of his accomplishments.

George Washington owed his mother far more than he may have realized. From her he got his physical strength and endurance, his resolution and determination, and his ambition to make his own way in life.

Mary Ball Washington's influence on the life of George Washington was greater than that of many other women. It was not, however, a better influence. It was not a pleasant influence. It was a character-building influence.

Sally Fairfax had taught George Washington to curb his passion, to use restraint, to substitute judgment for emotion. And difficult as this lesson was for him to accept in his personal relationship with Sally, George loved the teacher.

Eliza Powel urged Washington to continue to be active and use all his faculties to better his nation and to serve a second presidential term. George put aside his personal preference to retire to his home and take life easier. He accepted Eliza's urgings with undiminished respect and affection for this woman, his favorite adult female companion.

Betsy Fauntleroy taught Washington to face rejection; his marriage proposal was twice rejected. George Washington never spoke badly of her. He accepted this personally difficult lesson and influence on his life with no ill will toward Betsy.

In direct contrast, Mary Ball Washington's lessons which powerfully influenced his character traits of determination and resolution, of self-reliance, and of ambition to make his own way, were not accepted lovingly by George Washington. Those lessons had been expressed in tones of bitterness, resentment, and stubbornness. They had been pushed on him by a complaining, demanding, scornful, selfish person. Washington did not love this teacher, did not like her, probably came close to hating her. But because she was his mother, he did his duty, embarrassed by this woman and quite indifferent and unexpressive toward her.

The significance of Mary Ball Washington's influence on George Washington's life cannot be overstated.

8

Martha Parke Custis

SHE WAS GEORGE Washington's Sweet Innocent Girl.

Martha Parke Custis was the two-year-old daughter of George's bride, and already she had the affectionate nickname Patsy.

Born in 1756, the child was dark-haired, spindly and somewhat sickly right from the start. But little Patsy captured George Washington's heart totally when he first met her in 1758 at her mother's home. Patsy was an intriguing and happy child, whose story is both short and tragic.

At the time her father died, when she was only a year old, Patsy inherited securities and bonds. Her brother, Jackie, at age three, inherited from his father both land and tobacco crops.

After Martha's marriage to George Washington, Patsy immediately began to be pampered by George. He indulged her excessively. Every Christmas George Washington made sure she received a new doll baby and several items of fashionable clothes—little hats, gloves, dresses and shoes. When Patsy was four, George Washington ordered from London "clothes, toys, fans, masks and little books for children." George gave Patsy her own pony to ride. She had her own saddle, riding clothes, gloves, and pumps. And a favorite item was her very own pocket looking glass. Patsy even had her own maid, named Rose. When she was five years old, she was given a spinet and began to learn about music, dance, and the classics—all designed to help her become a lady.

Patsy was not a robust, healthy child from the beginning.

However, the first twelve years of her life seemed to be spent in happy pleasures, diversions and amusements, as well as in the learning process for a young girl in colonial America. At age twelve things changed dramatically. She began having fits. Epilepsy set in. Her nervous system was diseased and gradually would be destroyed.

The fits grew both more frequent and more severe. Patsy's condition got worse and worse. The fits would occur at any time, any place, without warning. The helplessness of those around her, especially her mother and George Washington, increased in direct proportion to the frequency of the seizures.

The best-known physicians were called to treat Patsy. Dr. Hugh Mercer of Fredericksburg, Virginia, was considered a foremost, knowledgeable doctor of epileptic patients, and he treated Patsy often. She was put into iron rings by February 1769 because the fits were so severe. No real relief came from all the treatments. George Washington vicariously suffered Patsy's pathetic illness and hurt as he watched doctor after doctor fail to relieve the condition.

Even during the months and years of these fits, Patsy continued to be trained and to travel. She belonged to a dancing group that met at various plantations in and around Fairfax County. The dancing group's master, named Christian, taught the girls and their young escorts the minuet, country dances, and dancing etiquette. The group met at Mount Vernon in 1770 when Patsy was fourteen.

Patsy traveled with George and Martha Washington to Williamsburg, Fredericksburg, Eltham, and other spots in Virginia. Although she was a delight and joy to have along, the parents constantly feared the onset of an epileptic seizure. The availability of medical assistance was a factor that had to be included in any travel plans.

On June 19, 1773, Patsy shared dinner with her family at Mount Vernon. The seventeen-year-old young lady was having an especially good time. George Washington wrote: "Patsy rose from dinner about 4 p.m. in better spirits than for some time. Shortly she was seized with one of her usual fits and expired in less than two minutes, without uttering a word, a groan, or scarce a sigh."

51

Her death was a shock and a grief. Martha Washington took it particularly hard. George Washington wrote: "This sudden and unexpected blow I scare need add has almost reduced my poor wife to the lowest ebb of misery."

George himself was more philosophical about the loss of his little love. He, at age forty-one, was a total realist about life's events. And after all the pain Patsy had endured for almost five years, and the suffering her condition had caused those who could only stand by helplessly, Patsy's death was somewhat of a relief. Her misery ended, she was headed for eternal rest. George Washington wrote: "The Sweet Innocent Girl entered into a more happy and peaceful abode."

Patsy never had known a young love, never had a marriage proposal, never even a steady beau. She had male friends and knew and enjoyed mixed company, but the young lady's life ended without the joys and the pains of a love affair. George Washington seemed to regret this omission in his Patsy's life experiences.

It was no consolation to him but it should be noted that George Washington inherited about £8,000 on Patsy's death. This sum was in securities and bonds.

9

Eleanor Parke Custis

TECHNICALLY, Eleanor Parke Custis ("Nelly") was George Washington's step-granddaughter. In human terms she was more a combination of (a) a replacement for his little love, Patsy, who had died at age seventeen in 1773; and (b) a full-fledged granddaughter for Grandpa to dote on.

Nelly, who rekindled George Washington's paternal instincts, was a major joy and delight in his life from the time she entered his household as a two-year-old until his death eighteen years later. From the time George Washington was forty-nine years old until his death at almost age sixty-eight, Nelly Custis lived as part of his family under his roof at Mount Vernon, Virginia.

Nelly's father, John Parke Custis, died in 1781. Nelly and her brother, George Washington Parke Custis, came to Mount Vernon to live with grandmother, Martha Washington, and step-grandfather, George Washington. Nelly's two sisters, Elizabeth Parke Custis and Martha Custis, continued to live with their mother, who subsequently married Dr. Stuart. Nelly and brother remained at Mount Vernon after the marriage.

So, Nelly Custis really knew only one home and one set of "parents" for the first twenty years of her life. She was raised fondly by doting grandparents, whose maturity offered both good training and material luxuries.

George Washington never had children of his own. When he married Martha in 1759, she had a son, Jackie, and a daughter, Patsy. Tragically, Patsy died when only seventeen years old, and

53

the void in George's life was felt deeply. Less than eight years later, granddaughter Nelly Custis came into his daily existence and partially filled that void. The things George Washington wanted to know and enjoy as Patsy grew up, would now be rerun with a healthier child and a much happier ending. His desires to help raise a young girl to become a lady and to see her comfortably and happily married would be fulfilled with the life of Nelly Custis.

But beginning anew the process at age forty-nine brought different emotions and a different thought process into operation. For example, George Washington would philosophize to Nelly Custis on matters of boys, love, and marriage. And he would teach her with more seriousness and more maturity than he could have shown while in his thirties. Furthermore, his prominence in the new federal government as president for eight of the eighteen years Nelly Custis lived in his household would put practical restrictions on his time and his freedom to play the role of parent to this girl. What he would and could teach Nelly Custis by example was somewhat stifled by formal state affairs, serious governmental policy discussions with visitors and dinner guests, and the need for the proper display of presidential dignity, reserve, and formality. John Adams judged that Nelly Custis got little liberty and was tied quite tightly to her grandmother's apron strings while George Washington was president.

The other role, that of "doting grandfather," shows up in several ways and most vividly during the six years from 1783-1789, when he was Farmer Washington, as Nelly Custis called her grandpa. This period lasted from the time she was four to ten years old and full of vigor and mischief. George Washington loved to take little Nelly along with him when he toured the acreage at Mount Vernon by coach, a trip his diary records as about fourteen miles. We can only imagine (history books do not authentically record) their talks as they shared the experiences of checking the tobacco crops, deciding which trees should be planted or moved to where, instructing the servants to begin various new projects, and similar details on the thousands of acres. And most likely they shared fun and laughter. Nelly Custis said of George Washington: "The grave dignity he usually wore did not prevent his keen enjoyment of a joke."

Nelly Custis was impulsive as a child but one who learned her lessons well. One time she went for a stroll on the grounds at Mount Vernon; it was after dark and Nelly went alone. Upon her return, Grandmother Martha began to scold her severely. Grandpa George intervened and came to Nelly's defense—he suggested that "maybe she was not alone!" Nelly did not appreciate this suggestion. Her feelings hurt, she told Grandpa Washington, "Yes, I was alone." She assured him that she had told grandmother that she was alone. "I am being honest," she said. Grandpa got the message loud and clear: his attempt to save Nelly from the scolding had backfired. He then apologized to Nelly for having doubted her word. After all, honesty was the important lesson, and Nelly Custis learned that one well.

Nelly was a talented young girl. She drew exceptionally well. One of her efforts that has been preserved, a drawing of a bird, shows a gifted eye and hand. Nelly Custis also made drawings of her grandparents that have been preserved through the years. She pictured Martha and George Washington in individual silhouettes in profile. And Nelly described herself at that period of time as "not very industrious, but I work a little, read, play the harpsichord, write and talk, and find my time fully taken up with these several employments."

A dark-haired girl, Nelly had good social graces and overall beauty. Henry Waney during a visit to Mount Vernon found himself staring at sixteen-year-old Nelly Custis. He said she was "a very pleasing, young lady. She has perfection of form, of color, of expression, of softness, and of firmness of mind."

Nelly Custis' youthful attitude toward boys amused George Washington. She said she was too busy for them and also that she never would give herself "a moment's uneasiness on account of any young man." In addition to amusing Washington, this attitude inspired him to set down for her benefit some of his own philosophy on love, sex, and marriage. On January 16, 1795, George Washington wrote to his sixteen-year-old granddaughter that: (1) "the

55

passions of your sex are easier raised than allayed"; (2) delicacy and custom prevent a lady from making any advances; (3) a lady should not be a flirt. "Nothing short of good sense and an easy unaffected conduct can draw the line between prudery and coquetry." (4) Nelly must always remember that "a sensible woman can never be happy with a fool"; and finally, (5) he wished Nelly a "good husband when you want and deserve one."

At age nineteen Nelly Custis was engaged to be married and knew what kind of a future life she wanted. She preferred to live "forever in the country" and spend her life "on a plantation." The cities, such as Philadelphia and Williamsburg, which she had come to know quite well, simply had no appeal for her. Her impressions of city life were undoubtedly molded by the formalities she saw in her grandfather's eight years of presidential homes, affairs of state, and the accompanying demands on his time and energies. Nelly decided she much preferred the life she knew at Mount Vernon. Here again, her conclusion was unquestionably formed by her precious memories of the days when Grandpa Washington had time to spend with her. Then he could and did teach her things she knew and cared about, and was her "Farmer Washington," a more relaxed, happy man.

Nelly Custis always found George Washington a fond comrade at Mount Vernon, and she loved him with total devotion. When it came time to set her wedding date, she chose February 22, 1799—Grandpa's sixty-seventh birthday!

Washington's diary records the wedding as follows: "Miss Custis was married abt. Candle light to Mr. Lawr. Lewis." Grandpa, not the groom, paid twenty dollars to the Reverend Mr. Thomas Davis for his services in performing the wedding of Nelly Custis to Major Lawrence Lewis at home in Mount Vernon.

For the wedding ceremony, Nelly wanted George Washington to wear a new uniform that was being prepared by a tailor. But this was not to be. Despite repeated prompting by Washington, the tailor delayed and delayed. The new uniform was not finished in time for the wedding. In fact, it was not even ready when Washington died ten months later. So, for the ceremony George

Washington put on his General's buff and blue uniform from the days of the Revolutionary War.

For a wedding gift, George Washington gave Nelly a harpsichord that cost over a thousand dollars and still is at Mount Vernon today, in playable condition. And to the new groom and his bride, Washington gave his assurances that their desired future life-style on a plantation would be fulfilled. He intended to leave for them by his last will and testament almost a thousand acres of farmland adjacent to Mount Vernon, together with a mill and distillery already on that property. (In his last will, written some five months later, Washington did exactly as he assured them he would.)

Interestingly, George Washington would not give the property to the couple until his death; he preferred to keep it in his own hands "in fairness to others" in the family. Aware that the couple might misunderstand, Washington made it clear that he had "no suspicion" that the couple would conduct themselves "in such a manner as to incur my serious displeasure." But a total realist George Washington always was. He was not about to willingly arrange title to his property while he was still alive in such a way that he might become embroiled in a marital dispute should the lovers decide to abandon their togetherness plans, which would incur Washington's "serious displeasure."

The couple, however, was permitted to begin to use the land immediately after their marriage, build a house on it, operate the mill and distillery, and pay a modest rental to George Washington for the privilege of doing so. If they changed their minds about the property while he was alive, he would reimburse them a fair amount for improvements and betterments to that property.

Less than three weeks before George Washington died, Nelly Custis Lewis gave birth to a baby girl, born on November 27, 1799. Martha Washington presented the new mother with a family heirloom, a black walnut crib for the infant. The crib is today on display at Mount Vernon.

Nelly's life was off to a good start by the time George Washington permanently left the scene by death on December 14, 1799. He must have known about, and taken great pride in, the way things were going for Nelly and how well she had developed by age twenty. His frustrated hopes for Patsy were amply fulfilled by Nelly.

10

Eliza (Mrs. Samuel) Powel

GEORGE WASHINGTON had, as an adult, many female social contacts. One lady, however, stands out far above all the rest as a true and valued close personal friend.

Eliza Powel and George Washington were friends for twenty-three years, from 1776 to his death in 1799. She was one of the very few people, male or female, who could ever tease George Washington. She could draw him out; could give frank, candid, confidential, personally meaningful advice and comments on a wide range of subjects; could thoroughly amuse and challenge him mentally. She could and did even banter with Washington about sex and about his restraint around women generally. Some historians conclude that Eliza Powel knew Washington more closely than any other woman except his wife, Martha. And in some ways Eliza was a more important companion to George than Martha was, specifically in his presidential years. By then Martha had become fully domesticated, a kind, grandmotherly person. Eliza Powel was still in the prime of life, with regard to age and social activity.

All during these twenty-three years, Eliza Powel was Mrs. Samuel Powel, a happily married matron in the highest levels of Philadelphia society. Her father was a financial mentor of Robert Morris. Her husband was among the wealthiest and most respected men in Philadelphia. He was part of the leading mercantile family of the city. And Martha Washington knew Eliza Powel well and confided in her frequently. The relationship of Eliza Powel and

George Washington was one of deep personal friendship; there is no hint of anything more. She was not his mistress.

Eliza Powel, who was ten years younger than Washington, was a saucy, interesting, attractive, intelligent, flirtatious woman. She was President Washington's confidante and advisor on several social questions. She had a high forehead, blue eyes, a shapely and well-defined nose, a full and firm mouth, a rounded and pleasant face. She was the epitome of confidence, determination and class. Always dressed in the latest fashions, in the best taste, Eliza Powel was an asset at social events, always correct, proper and charming. She was also clever and gay but did have some tendencies, particularly after age fifty, toward being too talkative, too sensitive to critics, too anxious to charm. She was said by one acquaintance to judge people by how closely and well they listened to her. She was fluent and George Washington was not. A good listener he was, however, and she liked that trait.

Eliza frequently had spells of depression, melancholy, morbidness. She excused herself from a dinner party at Mount Vernon in 1787 because she felt that her presence at the table was depressing to the others. In some aspects, Eliza Powel's personality was a paradox in public. But in private and to George Washington, she was what he needed most, truly his favorite female companion during the years of his presidency.

The Washingtons and the Powels were neighbors in Philadelphia in 1776, in 1783, and in the presidential years of 1789-1797. The Powels visited at Mount Vernon, Virginia, in the fall of 1787. Eliza and Samuel Powel owned an estate in the center of Philadelphia, a show place with four mansions, rambling gardens, walks lined with fine statuary, and in George Washington's words "a profusion of lemon, orange, and citron trees." By comparison, Mount Vernon was little more than a simple, rural farmhouse. George Washington fully enjoyed the splendor at the Powels' estate, and he liked to visit there frequently. It was a great place to relax, sip tea, and chat about everything from governmental policy to raising the grandchildren. The place was relaxing and pleasant, but the real attraction for Washington was Eliza Powel.

She seemed always to have, or was willing to make, the time to entertain George Washington. She would argue with him about a sticky point of policy being considered by the new federal government. Eliza Powel discussed such matters intelligently and playfully. Washington seemed to find her an invaluable sounding board for ideas. One time she sent President Washington a pamphlet that contained ideas she felt were dangerous. Washington assured her that the pamphlet had not given him a "moment's painful sensation" and then signed the letter "with very great esteem, regard and affection."

She knew his character so well that he trusted her judgment and relied on her insight and interpretations. And she bantered with him in a most pleasant and amusing way; she challenged his wit, his mentality, his ponderings.

In November, 1792, George Washington was pondering whether to quit the presidency at the end of one term or stand for a second term. Eliza Powel was consulted. After he confided in her and she gave the subject thought, she then wrote a long, strong, persuasive letter expressing her conclusion that he must not step down down—he must serve a second term. Her letter showed an astute appraisal of both the public sentiment toward Washington and her own analysis of him and his personal needs.

Eliza Powel's letter made five main arguments why President Washington must serve a second term:

First, his resignation would be a disaster for millions. She intentionally avoided any discussion of the sectional and political overtones brewing about Washington's performance during his first term. She concentrated on the nation as a whole.

Second, a refusal to serve a second term would be criticized on the grounds that he "would take no further risks." She suggested it would be said that George Washington foresaw the collapse of the ship of state and that the captain was the first to jump overboard and off the sinking ship. A resignation would be seen as a fundamental weakness of both the new nation and of George Washington because when the going "got rough," the leader quit and ran home.

Third, George Washington's well-known sensibility to public opinion would be "torn from you by the envious and malignant" by a resignation. Eliza Powel herself was vulnerable to criticism—she could not personally accept it at all—and she knew that Washington was of the same temperament, capable of being deeply wounded by critical comments.

Fourth, Eliza saw in Washington's indecision about a second term a recurrence of his innate lack of confidence in his own talents and capabilities. This trait, whether called reserve or shyness or humility or whatever, appears repeatedly in his career. He never felt up to any task he was asked to do, whether to lead the revolutionary army or lead the new nation. Eliza Powel faced this aspect directly, and sternly told George Washington that he must "overcome the diffidence of your abilities."

Fifth, Eliza hit George with a personally powerful argument: he was not infirm, he was able and useful, not ready to be taken off center stage and put out into the wings. She urged him to continue to employ all his faculties on those duties which "elevate and fortify the soul." His personal self-respect, pride, and pleasure, as well as his lifelong sense of dedication to civic duty, demanded that he continue in office for a second term. With this potent personal argument, Eliza Powel closed by urging her dear friend to stay on. Such an argument could be presented to George Washington only by such a close confidante who knew him extremely well.

Washington did not reply to Eliza's letter in writing. We are not sure he ever discussed the subject with her any further. In any event, George Washington did accept the call and did serve another term as president of the United States.

Important as this aspect was—that of serious governmental matters—the truer value of Eliza Powel to George Washington was in the realm of the personal.

She gave him an opportunity to unwind and get away from affairs of state and into an atmosphere of comfort and true, undemanding friendship. She could tease him as a "private gentleman." And here at her home in Philadelphia, Washington could ask Eliza Powel, in 1798, to buy a present for his step-granddaughter, Nelly Custis. George said she could spend "30 or 60 or more dollars on a handsome muslin or anything else that is not the whim of the day." And Washington added that Eliza might help further: "Is there anything not of much cost I could carry to Mrs. Washington as a momento that she has not been forgotten?"

Eliza Powel could draw George Washington out about his attitude toward sex. She kidded him about his exceptional restraint around women, his "continence," as she termed it. Through all the Washington reserve, dignity, and propriety, he is reported to have been able to tell Eliza Powel that he was less concerned about being caught in adultery than in betraying the confidence of a lady. She brought out his sense of humor and wit in a way few others were ever able to do. His confidence in her was tremendous. He could trust her with his innermost thoughts and feelings—what a unique and untypical thing for George Washington to be able to do. And what a unique and unusual woman Eliza Powel was to be able to fill this need.

Martha Washington, too, could and did confide in Eliza Powel. Martha, for example, asked advice on how to train her granddaughters to become society belles and real ladies. Eliza sent Martha some special collars for the girls to wear to keep their necks up. It would teach them to walk erect and to throw back their shoulders which "expands the chest" and prevents the "foolishly bashful look" so many of the young girls mistakenly tried to cultivate.

On December 7, 1796, Eliza Powel sent to Martha Washington a remedy for George's indigestion. Her instructions were that George was to "take a glass on his return from Congress. I know his sensitivity, diffidence, and delicacy too well not to believe that his spirit will not be a little agitated on the solemn, and I fear, last occasion that he will take of addressing his fellow citizens."

When George Washington was ready to retire permanently to his beloved Mount Vernon, he could not bring himself to say good-bye to Eliza Powel in person. So he wrote her a letter, and he gave her a valued item: his personal desk. Eliza replied with flirtatiousness and lightness. She wrote George that in the desk she had found a neatly tied package of love letters from "a Lady" addressed to him. After writing more and really milking this tempting little morsel of potential scandal for several sentences, Eliza gave in and confessed to George that the love letters were all from his wife, Martha! Please, what did he want her to do with them?

George Washington replied, in what has to be one of his wittiest writings, that if he had love letters to lose, Eliza's long preambles were to see "how far my nerves were able to sustain the shock of having betrayed the confidence of a lady." Washington then added that if Eliza Powel were to have peeked into those love letters from Martha Washington, she would have seen them "more fraught with expressions of friendship than of enamoured love. A reader of the 'romantic order' could only have given the sheets warmth by setting them on fire."

What a precious and delightful relationship Eliza Powel and George Washington knew. They could tease and laugh and level barbs at each other. They could also fully explore serious topics together. And they could be open and frank about it all—Samuel Powel never intervened, never objected, never took offense. And Martha Washington was known to have copied some of George's preliminary thoughts to Eliza and put them into letters in signable form for George to read and sign and send. Just imagine—his wife acting as his secretary for correspondence with his favorite female companion!

A most remarkable lady, this Eliza Powel. All the more so because she was a warm, personal, longtime, influential friend of George Washington's.

11

Eight Other Women

THIS CHAPTER DISCUSSES eight other ladies who were of significant importance in the overall story of George Washington's women. Six of them were relatives; two were associates who touched Washington's life in a material way.

Mildred Washington——sister of George Washington. Born on June 21, 1739, when her brother was seven years old. George's association with his baby sister was extremely brief. She died in infancy on October 28, 1740.

Elizabeth Washington——sister of George Washington. Born on June 30, 1733, when George was one year and four months old. Known and referred to by George Washington as "Betty," she married Mr. Lewis. Betty Lewis is mentioned in Washington's last will and testament as "my deceased sister Betty Lewis." She died in March 1797.

Sarah Washington——daughter of George Washington's half-brother, Lawrence. She was the direct inheritor of the Mount Vernon mansion and property, when Lawrence died in 1752. It was a short-term holding. She died less than two months after Lawrence did, and George Washington then took over Mount Vernon.

Fanny Bassett Washington——wife of George Augustine Washington, who was George Washington's nephew. The nephew and wife, Fanny, lived at Mount Vernon, dined frequently with Martha and George, and were virtually members of the closest part of Washington's household. Fanny was a true, dear friend, and her husband was a trusted and valued manager of the Mount Vernon property until 1793.

Elizabeth Parke Custis——Nicknamed "Betey," she was an older sister of Nelly Custis. Betey was George Washington's step-granddaughter, who continued to live with her mother after her father's death in 1781. Nelly had gone to live at Mount Vernon with grandmother Martha and step-grandfather, George Washington. When Betey's mother was married for the second time (to Dr. David Stuart), Betey lived with them. She hated it. She found Dr. Stuart "morose." Apparently a sensitive and nervous girl, Betey was so shy that when George Washington visited at the Stuarts' home, she could not bring herself to walk out to greet her step-grandfather, the president of the United States. Betey, also on that occasion, could not eat anything at the dinner table. Biographers have indicated that Betey was envious of her sister's life under George Washington's roof; by comparsion, her own lot in life seemed less attractive and less fun to a young girl.

When Betey was seventeen years old, she opened her heart to George Washington. She said she was not interested in boys and she "scorned" love. Then she directed her romantic attitude to her step-grandfather. She asked him to please send a miniature portrait she could wear as a necklace around her neck, "next to my breast." George Washington took up his pen and on September 14, 1794, wrote a lengthy letter to Betey. In it he set forth some of his views on love and marriage and what it was all about. Washington's letter cautioned her not to "look for perfect felicity before you consent to wed." Betey should not expect a love affair to bring heaven down to the earth. "Love is a mighty pretty thing," wrote George Washington, "but it is cloying, and when the first transports of the passion begin to subside, which it assuredly will do . . . it serves to evince that love is too dainty a food to live upon alone . . ."

Washington suggested to Betey the three essential ingredients for a happy marriage: the marriage partner should possess "good sense, good dispositions, and the means of supporting you in the way you have been brought up."

Very shortly after receiving this letter, Betey wrote George Washington that she was engaged. She planned to marry Thomas Law, an Englishman, a widower, a man almost twice her age.

George Washington was taken aback. He had known and heard some unfavorable things about Mr. Law. He was a bit stunned at the announcement and not very happy. Most of all, he seemed to be hurt by Betey's failure to confide in him about her feelings for Thomas Law. He expected she would have discussed the matter with him earlier and heard his views about the man. George Washington reminded Betey "you know how much I love you." Even though Washington had grave reservations about the proposed marriage, he gave approval on the basis that Betey knew her own heart and mind. Betey and Thomas Law lived in Washington, D.C., where he was a real estate investor and speculator. The marriage turned out to be a disaster.

Martha Parke Custis——a third step-granddaughter of George Washington, who also lived with her mother, Dr. David Stuart, and her older sister, Betey. Interestingly, Martha did exactly what Betey did—she married a man named Thomas, who owned and operated a real estate business in the District of Columbia. But her marriage to Thomas Peter turned out to be much happier and more successful than was Betey's.

Oney Judge——A black servant girl at Mount Vernon. George Washington said that he and his wife raised her almost as if she were their own child. Oney was a skilled seamstress who is recorded to have sewn hour by hour, day after day, sitting with Martha Washington in the parlor.

One day a Frenchman visited at Mount Vernon and began talking seriously with Oney Judge. A short time later both disappeared. Martha Washington guessed that they had eloped. But she feared he would get her pregnant and then desert her with no money, no home, nothing.

George Washington wrote to Joseph Whipple, the customs collector at Portsmouth, New Hampshire, where Oney Judge was reported to be staying. He asked Whipple to arrange for Oney to be put on the next boat headed toward Alexandria, Virginia. After all, Oney Judge was property of George Washington, his household slave/servant. But Oney Judge was now in New Hampshire, a northern state—an anti-slavery state. Whipple was not so sure he could just up and put her on a boat. So he presented two aspects for George Washington to consider: (1) after investigation of the entire situation, including discussions with Oney Judge herself, with others in the black community, and with unidentified sources, Whipple had determined to his own complete satisfaction that Oney Judge had not been taken from Mount Vernon by a seducer. She had simply taken this opportunity to run for her own freedom from slavery; her motive was "a thirst for freedom." (2) Furthermore, whether George Washington believed that determination or not, it would set off "rioting" in the streets if Whipple were to press the issue of Oney Judge's return to Mount Vernon. He would not force Oney Judge to return unless George Washington sent him something in writing from the attorney general of the United States. Oney Judge remained free; George Washington dropped the situation without further word.

Henrietta Liston——the Scottish wife of the new British minister, Robert Liston, who arrived in Philadelphia in 1796. The Listons were a delightful couple, whom the Washingtons quickly took to as personal friends. Mrs. Liston's blond hair was beginning to show some white, but her complexion remained youthful, fresh, and delicate. She was attractive. Mrs. Liston was quite impressed with the old hero of the Revolution. President George Washington found that he could open his personal emotions and memories to Mrs. Liston.

Henrietta Liston was more objective in her views of George Washington, than, for example, his dear friend of that same city at that same time, Mrs. Eliza Powel. Mrs. Liston's memoirs record some incisive impressions of George Washington. She noted that she expected him to be a much more aggressive, fiery, stirred-up individual than he was; it was hard for her to understand how such a reserved, reticent man as George Washington could have had such a memorable, demanding career, especially during the passionate years of the Revolutionary War. Mrs. Liston also accused George Washington of having a "cold heart."

Henrietta Liston wrote three other items about George Washington:

(1) His "first and last pleasure" and consuming interest was in farming. He loved to discuss it, do it, and reminisce about it; and he kept current on every new development in farming and farm management.

(2) Letter writing seemed to be his forte. "His style was plain, correct, nervous." He was not fluent as a speaker or even as an informal conversationalist; he expressed himself best and most comfortably in writing, on both the high governmental level and in correspondence with friends and relatives.

(3) George Washington had such "perfect good breeding." He seemed always to be correct and proper. He had tremendous knowledge, or instinct, for what was tasteful, right, of long-lasting and fully acceptable value for future generations. This was most evident in his actions as first president of the United States, when he set the tone for the office and set procedures that have stood the test of time—they have been willingly followed by every person who has served as president since Washington served. It was virgin territory when George Washington walked the path of the presidency for eight years, and Mrs. Liston was amazed and perplexed about this performance by him—she kept asking herself, silently and out loud, how could a man from his background possibly have achieved this high degree of "perfect good breeding"?

Gossip was heavy about Henrietta Liston at the time Washington was finishing his second presidential term. She wept openly and excessively. Stories circulated that the relationship was more than had previously been thought—why else would this lady be so upset by George Washington's departure from Philadelphia and his return to a place miles away, Mount Vernon, Virginia? No reliable answers are found. One widely accepted theory is that this lady from a far-off country would sincerely and deeply miss the brief but strong personal acceptance, friendliness, and courtesies Washington showed. He was a true friend to the "newcomers." He had made her life in this new country pleasant and easier.

And Mrs. Henrietta Liston appreciated what George Washington had done as president of the United States. She wrote that "he had for eight years sacrificed his natural taste, first habits, and early propensities—I believe we may truly say—solely to what he thought the good of his country."

12

Nineteen More Women

ONE MEASURE OF THE esteem in which a person holds another is to see the name specifically mentioned in the last will and testament. By use of this measure alone, the names of nineteen additional women show up as being held in high regard by George Washington.

Washington's last will and testament was entirely in his own handwriting. It was dated July 9, 1799, and admitted to probate on January 20, 1800. It begins with an identification of himself: "I George Washington of Mount Vernon, a citizen of the United States, and lately President of the same . . ." And each time he mentions the name of a beneficiary, he includes a description that identifies that person. Some descriptions show the family relationship, others show where the person lived.

A term evidencing affection appears only by the name of one beneficiary, Martha Washington. George identified her as "my dearly beloved wife, Martha Washington." And in the preparatory sentences to his devise to Eleanor Parke (Nelly) Custis, his stepdaughter who lived with George Washington at Mount Vernon from age two to twenty, Washington makes it plain that he thought of her as his own; but he identified Nelly as a "grandchild of my wife."

The last will mentions the names of twenty-four women. Five of these women are covered in fuller detail in other chapters of this book. Those five names and Washington's description of each are as follows:

(1) "my dearly beloved wife, Martha Washington."
(2) "Eleanor Parke Custis, grandchild of my wife."
(3) "my deceased sister Betty Lewis."
(4) Elizabeth Parke Law and (5) Martha Parke Peter are listed as beneficiaries in George Washington's last will. No distinct identification is made by Washington; they were his two other step-grandaughters, who continued to live with their mother after their father died in 1781 and after her marriage to Dr. David Stuart.

In addition to these five women, George Washington mentions nineteen more women in his last will. They are in two separate aspects of the will. First, the will makes "specific devises" to and names the following ten women:

Mary "widow of Bartholomew Dandridge (my wife's brother)."
"my neice [sic] Betty Lewis."
"my sister in law Hannah Washington and Mildred Washington."
"my friends Eleanor Stuart, Hannah Washington of Fairfax and Elizabeth Washington of Hayfield."
"Sally B. Haynie (a distant relative of mine)."
"Sarah Green daughter of the deceased Thomas Bishop."
"Ann Walker daughter of Jno. Alton."

The second aspect of his last will covers the "more important parts of my Estate." Here George Washington names and identifies nine additional women, as follows:

"Elizabeth Spotswood, Jane Thornton and Ann Ashton, daughters of my deceased brother Augustine Washington."
"Betty Carter, daughter of my deceased sister Betty Lewis."
"Harriet Park, daughter of my deceased brother Samuel Washington."
"Jane Washington, daughter of my deceased brother John Augustine Washington."
"Frances Ball and Mildred Hammond, daughters of my brother Charles Washington."
"Maria Washington, daughter of my deceased nephew Geo. Augustine Washington."

So, from the last will and testament of George Washington, we discover the names of nineteen other women for whom he showed some measure of concern.

However, biographers and historians have largely ignored these nineteen names as having little significant influence on Washington's life. Surely each of the nineteen had some impact on his life; he did remember them and did give each a portion of his total estate assets. But these nineteen women should not be considered as a major part of George Washington's life, his loves, his female companions.

They are included in the subject matter of *George Washington's Women* because they are part of the total picture. As a group, they were held in esteem by him. And each of the nineteen must have meant something special to George Washington.

13

And—Finally—113 Additional Women

W EBSTER'S NEW WORLD DICTIONARY defines *diary* as "a daily written record, expecially of the writer's own experiences, thoughts, etc."

George Washington's handwritten diary was compiled and published in 1925 in a four-volume set. The set covers the years from 1748 to 1799, from the time he was sixteen years old until his death at age sixty-seven. But this diary compilation shows periods when a diary was not kept or is now missing. It turns out that there are gaps totalling almost thirty of the fifty-one years. So, we really have a daily written record of George Washington's own experiences, thoughts, etc., for only twenty-one years of his adult life.

In his diary are mentioned the names of at least 113 women who are not discussed elsewhere in this book. These 113 names include: infants, children, teenagers, adult ladies, and old women. They were dinner guests, house guests, and visitors to Mount Vernon and other houses where Washington stayed. Some of these women were hostesses to George Washington during his travels, female companions for short trips to church and nearby towns, escorts to dances, parties, and dinners. And some were the wives of the most distinguished names in the Revolutionary War and in the new federal government.

Most of these 113 women mentioned in George Washington's

diary are not identified by him. Occasionally, he would write that one person was the child of *X,* or that Mr. *X* and his "Lady" were present. He might use some other descriptive term, but usually he merely set down the woman's name.

The first name of a woman that appears in George Washington's diary is in an entry for November 6, 1751:

". . . Received . . . an invitation from Mrs. Clarke and Miss Roberts to come and see the (display of fireworks)." The editor of Washington's diary identified Miss Roberts as a niece of Mrs. Clarke, but there is no identification of Mrs. Clarke.

The last entry in Washington's diary mentioning a woman's name is on December 11, 1799 (three days before his death):

". . . Lord Fairfax, his son Thos. and daughter, Mrs. Warner Washington . . . dined here. . . ."

In between the first name of Mrs. Clarke and the last name of Mrs. Warner Washington, were found 111 other women's names, exactly as shown in George Washington's diary. The following listing omits any reference to the same name appearing in several diary entries—such duplications are not counted:

1751

Miss Roberts
Mrs. Saturo Maynard

1760

Mrs. Sarah Barnes
Anna Marie Dandridge
Mrs. Bassett
Darcus, a negro servant
Betty, a negro servant
Phillis, a negro servant
Mrs. John Possey
Mrs. Joseph Chew
Mrs. Charles Green

Mrs. John Carlyle
Hannah Fairfax
Elizabeth Dent

1768

Miss Nicholas
Miss Betsey Ramsay
Miss Teresa Diggers
Miss Betty Diggers
Mrs. Elizabeth Dawson
Mrs. Richard Charlton
Miss Lettice Corbin
Mrs. West
Mrs. Seldon
Mrs. Mary Lee
Mrs. Henry Lee
Miss Sally Ballendine
Mrs. Manley

1769

Betsey Dandridge
Nancy Bassett
Mrs. Campbell
Mrs. Dalton
Miss Terrett
Mrs. Vobe

1770

Sally Carlyle
Betty Dalton
Milly Hunter
Miss Elizabeth Bronaugh
Mrs. Edward Ambler
Miss Elizabeth French
Miss Peggy Massey

Miss Nelly Marbray
Miss Nancy Peake

1771

Miss Nancy McCarty
Miss Molly Manly
Polly Brazier
Miss Mason
Miss Scott
Miss Fanny Eldridge

1773

Miss Reed
Miss Terrett
Mrs. Ann Slaughter

1774

Miss Ellzey
Mrs. Blackburn

1775

Mrs. Newman

1785

Mrs. William Grayson
Mrs. Moylan
Mrs. Fendel
Miss Flora Lee
Mrs. Samuel Hanson

1786

Mrs. Crawford
Mrs. Lyle

Mrs. Joseph Craik
Mrs. Jenifer
Mrs. Mordecai Throckmorton
Miss Conttee
Mrs. Edmund Randolph
Mrs. Jno. Mercer
Polly Blackburne

1787

Mrs. Mary Whitbey
Mrs. Samuel Meridith
Mrs. Richard Bache
Mrs. Potts

1788

Mrs. Roger West
Mrs. William Thompson
Miss Muir
Mrs. Herbert
Mrs. George Platter
Mrs. O'Connor

1789

Mrs. William Duer
Mrs. Tanner Haviland
Miss Cornelia Clinton
Mrs. John Jay
Mrs. Henry Knox
Mrs. Nathanael Greene
Mrs. Oliver Wolcott
Mrs. John Adams
Mrs. Richard Varick
Mrs. Thomas T. Tucker
Mrs. Robert R. Livingston

1790

Miss Anne Brown
Mrs. William Cushing
Mrs. Samuel Osgood
Mrs. Samuel Griffin
Mrs. Issac Coles
Mrs. Alexander White
Mrs. Thomas Jefferson
Mrs. Alexander Hamilton
Mrs. Tobias Lear

1797

Mrs. Tomson Mason
Mrs. Forest
Mrs. Henry Marchant
Miss Armistead
Miss Fitzhugh

1798

Mrs. Rosameh White

1799

Mrs. Boies
Miss Eaglin
Mrs. Presley Thornton
Mrs. Howell Lewis
Mrs. Carrington

It should be noted that a diary of George Washington is missing or was not kept by him, during three most important periods of time:

(a) The first period covers almost thirteen years. There is no diary available for April 14, 1748, to September 27, 1751; March 5,

1752 to October 30, 1753; June 28, 1754, to January 1, 1760; May 23, 1760, to May 23, 1761; October 23, 1761, to March 1, 1763; and, October 19, 1764, to December 31, 1764. This period covered much of his premarriage adult life and a large portion of the total years up to the time George Washington was age thirty-two.

(b) The second period covers almost ten years. No diary is found for the times from June 20, 1775, to May 1, 1781, and again from November 6, 1781, to September 1, 1784. This was the period during of the Revolutionary War and covers most of the time Washington was traveling as General of the Armies.

(c) The third major period covers about five years. There is no diary for the time from March 11, 1790, to June 1, 1791; July 5, 1791, to September 29, 1794; and from October 21, 1794, to April 13, 1795. These were the early years of Washington's presidency of the United States.

How many more women would have been named during these twenty-eight years is impossible to determine. It is, however, a safe assumption, based on his habits and practices, that George Washington would have noted the names of scores of other women in his personal diary if one had been kept.

A person's personal diary can be as complete or as secretive as that person prefers it to be. George Washington's diary for the earlier years is full of very brief daily entries; often only three or four words cover the entire daily record. Examples:

November 14, 1751——"At our Lodgings."

December 27, 1751——"Moderate Wind & Sea."

April 25, 1760——"Waited upon the Gov'r."

In the later portions of his diary, Washington often wrote at considerable length about a particular day. His entry for September 30, 1794, contains 219 words, and the entry for October 13, 1794, contains 398 words.

The fact that George Washington mentioned the names of these 113 women in his personal diary suggests they were of some meaningful and memorable experience and thought to him. Although they were not of particular, significant influence in Washington's life, these 113 women deserve to be listed in a book such as this to get the full picture of George Washington's women.

14

Was George Washington Sterile?

IN 1958, IN 1965, IN 1976, and again in 1977, three separate writers directly faced the question of whether George Washington was sterile. The conclusion of each, based on years of research, analysis, and probabilities, was affirmative—yes, George Washington was indeed sterile.

He most likely became sterile at age nineteen after suffering several severe illnesses of ague, pleurisy and smallpox. He had contracted smallpox on the only trip he ever made outside the United States, when he went to Barbados in 1751. Medically, smallpox alone at that time could well have caused sterility. And more surely the combination of these several illnesses might render a young male's body sterile in 1751.

George Washington had no children of his own, even though he and his wife, Martha, apparently wanted them and even though Martha had previously given birth to four babies.

One of his biographers suggests that Washington was rendered sterile at a youthful age in order to be prepared for his lasting and perpetual fatherhood, the role of Father of His Country.

It has also been suggested that his sterility made it possible for him to accept the life-risking military role he played in the revolution. The gist of this idea is that, since he had no direct natural heirs, his continuing presence on this earth was not as important to himself as it may have been if he had had young lives—part of his own body—directly dependent on him. And so it is suggested that George Washington, because he was sterile himself, tended to view one individual's life generally as less precious than a worthwhile cause. Therefore, he could more easily order soldiers into fatal battle.

Regardless of the plausibility and strength of these suggestions, it appears to this writer that George Washington's sterile state did bear directly on his attitude toward women.

He had the strongest and most rewarding relationships with those women who were charming, intelligent, wealthy, vivacious, and lively, regardless of their motherhood status.

The greatest and most passionate love of his life, Sally Fairfax, never had any children of her own.

Martha Washington, who never bore him any children during their marriage, was nonetheless fully and deeply loved and fondly treated by George Washington for over forty years.

Eliza Powel's influence and friendship for twenty years was not affected in the least by whether she had children or not. She was a complete, important, separate female in his life, one with whom he had the highest and closest personal rapport. And remember—it was Eliza Powel who could and did tease George Washington about his lifelong "continence" around women. Did she know all too well why he could restrain his vigorous, physically attractive body so fully and so easily?

And yet, George Washington never loved his own mother; in fact, he never even really liked her. The woman who bore him was not his kind of person, and she was simply not his friend. He largely ignored her for almost thirty years of his adult life, after having argued with her for at least ten years before that.

His widely accepted physical attraction to Polly Philipse, who he thought would surely produce healthy children, was not a strong enough factor to overcome a hesitancy about the total relationship. This delayed George Washington from asking her to be his bride until, clearly, such a request was too late—she was already engaged to another man. Maybe (if he knew then, at age twenty-four, that he was sterile) he was only paying lip service to the thought of healthy children with Polly. Or maybe, if he did not at that time know that he was sterile, we have a subconscious explanation for his overall hesitancy in that relationship. Polly Philipse said Washington was "no lover."

Postscript

During the period of research in preparing for this book, I frequently saw the recurrence of strongly worded comments to the
net effect that George Washington used women for social diver-
sion, for companionship, for the lighter side of his life—comments
that indicated, if not actually said, that Washington looked down
on women and minimized their impact on his life. The conclusion
was then drawn that he really did not need women to inspire or
push him into greatness. He was pictured as a total person within
himself, a person fundamentally uninfluenced by women. He was a
man's man, in a man's world.

These comments were found most often in books published
between 1800 and 1900. But past writers, including those in the
twentieth century, had not put together a complete picture of all the
important relationships Washington had with women. An isolated
account of a particular situation that fitted into the story then being
told was used to generalize. There was found no attempt to con-
solidate and evaluate, as a total, all his relationships over the years.
Doing that job was my purpose.

And so during the period of analyzing, outlining, and writing
this book, I have repeatedly discovered patterns that developed in
his relationships with women from early manhood to his last days.
These patterns leave little doubt that he was indeed profoundly influenced by the important women in his life: patterns that show a
molding process in this man; patterns that help explain how he built
such powerful personality traits; patterns that shed new insight into
his character, morals and reputation; patterns that force the
ultimate conclusion that George Washington was indeed a most

human person. He was a man who knew emotions, passions, love, and disappointments; a man who did not take lightly his relationships with women at any point in his life; a man who, rather than looking down on women, treated them and thought of them as at least his equal and probably as somewhat more than that.

He did not put women on a pedestal. He did put them into his life, romantically, meaningfully, purposefully, tenderly, and significantly. The strengths he got from several relationships certainly did influence him and did help him achieve greatness. The overall impact of George Washington's women was positive, favorable, and of deep and lasting significance to him. He was fortunate to know so many interesting and different women who, each in her own way, left a mark on him and who *in toto* were so important in his life. Tracing the influences of these women helps understand this man all the more.

Bibliography

Serious students of the life of George Washington have available the comparatively recent, excellent works of two eminent scholars. Their works attest to their dedication, industry, and talents. Douglas Southall Freeman's seven-volume biography *George Washington* is in the definitive form. It is thoroughly researched, documented, and authenticated. It earned the author the Pulitzer Prize. And James Thomas Flexner soon thereafter authored a four-volume biography, which won a Special Pulitzer Prize, and a superb one-volume book, *George Washington: The Indispensable Man.* Flexner concentrated on George Washington as a living, breathing human being.

These twelve volumes authoritatively cover the life of this remarkable American. Together they render much prior material inadequate and obsolete. (In 1965 Flexner calculated there were 2,997 cards in the New York Public Library pertaining to publications about George Washington.) But, these twelve volumes present the latest information and interpretations based on better, more extensive, and more imaginative research than had ever been done before.

The writer gratefully acknowledges the value and usefulness of these monumental works.

In preparing this book, scores of other publications were read and analyzed to gain guidance about and insight into the subject matter. No small part of the total effort was the writer's private collection of Washingtonia. This collection includes books, busts, postage stamps, coins and medals, wall plates and placques, cups, mugs, thimbles—virtually any item at all that features George

Washington. Many parts of the collection are described in the author's other book, *George Washington: Vignettes and Memorabilia,* Dorrance & Co., Inc., Philadelphia, 1977.

The following is a list of all publications referred to in preparation of this book. (The writer's private collection includes a copy of each):

Ambler, Charles H. *George Washington and the West.* New York: Russell & Russell, 1971.

Andrist, Ralph K. *George Washington: A Biography in His Own Words.* Vols. 1 and 2. New York: Newsweek Books, 1972.

Andrist, Ralph K. *George Washington: A Biography in His Own Words.* New York: Harper & Row, 1972.

Baker, W.S. *Medallic Portraits of Washington.* Philadelphia: Robert M. Lindsay Co., 1885.

Borden, Morton. *George Washington.* Englewood Cliffs, New Jersey: Prentice-Hall, 1969.

Borreson, Mary Jo. *Let's Go to Mount Vernon.* New York: G.P. Putnam's Sons, 1962.

Brockett, F.L. *The Lodge of Washington.* Alexandria, Virginia: George E. French, Publisher, 1876.

Buhler, Kathryn C. *Mount Vernon Silver.* Mount Vernon, Va.: The Mount Vernon Ladies Association of the Union, 1957.

Callahan, North. *George Washington: Soldier and Man.* New York: William Morrow & Co., 1972.

Commins, Saxe. *Basic Writings of George Washington.* New York: Random House, 1948.

Conkling, Margaret C. *Lives of Mary and Martha Washington.* Auburn, New York: Derby, Miller & Co., 1850.

Cunliffe, Marcus. *George Washington: Man and Monument.* New York: New America Library, 1958.

Cunliffe, Marcus. *George Washington and the Making of a Nation.* New York: American Heritage Publishing Co., 1966.

Custis, George Washington Parke. *Memoirs of Washington.* New York: Union Publishing House, 1859.

Davis, Burke. *George Washington and the American Revolution.* New York: Random House, 1975.

Decatur, Stephen, Jr. *Private Affairs of George Washington.* Cambridge, Mass.: Riverside Press, 1933.

DuPuy, Trevor Nevitt. *The Military Life of George Washington: American Soldier.* New York: Franklin Watts, 1969.

Eaton, Jeanette. *Leader By Destiny: George Washington Man & Patriot.* New York: Harcourt, Brace & Co., 1938.

Fede, Helen Maggs. *Washington Furniture at Mount Vernon.* Mount Vernon, Va.: The Mount Vernon Ladies Association of the Union, 1966.

Fitzpatrick, John C. *The Diaries of George Washington.* Vols. 1, 2, 3, 4. New York: Houghton Mifflin Co., 1925.

Fitzpatrick, John C. *George Washington: Colonial Traveller 1732-1775.* Indianapolis: The Bobbs-Merrill Co., 1927.

Fitzpatrick, John C. *The Last Will and Testament of George Washington,* Mount Vernon, Va.: The Mount Vernon Ladies Association of the Union, 1972.

Flexner, James Thomas. *George Washington.* Vols. 1, 2, 3, 4. Boston: Little, Brown & Co., 1965-1969.

Flexner, James Thomas. *Washington: The Indispensable Man.* Boston: Little, Brown & Co., 1974.

Freeman, Douglas Southall. *George Washington.* Seven vols. (Vol. 7 by John Alexander Carroll and Mary Wells Ashworth). New York: Charles Scribner's Sons, 1948-1957.

Friedel, Frank & Aikman, Lonnelle. *George Washington: Man and Monument.* Washington, D.C.: Washington National Monument Association, 1965.

Friedel, Frank. *Our Country's President.* Washington, D.C.: National Geographic Society, 1966.

Frothingham, Thomas C. *Washington: Commander in Chief.* New York: Houghton Mifflin Co., 1930.

Glass, Francis. *A Life of George Washington.* Washington, D.C.: George Washington University Press (in Latin prose with a grammatical and historical supplement), 1976 (reprint of 1835 publication).

Hatch, Charles E., Jr. *Yorktown and the Siege of 1781.* National Park Service Historical Handbook Series, No. 14, 1954 (Revised 1957).

Haworth, Paul Leland. *George Washington: Farmer.* Indianapolis: Bobbs-Merrill Co., 1915.

Headley, J.T. *Washington and His Generals,* Vols. 1 and 2, New York: A.L. Burt Co., c. 1857.

Headley, J.T. *Washington and His Generals.* Vol. 2. New York: Hurst & Co., c. 1857.

Heaton, Ronald E. *Valley Forge: Yesterday and Today.* Norristown, Pa: Privately published, 1960.

Henley, Leonard. *Life of George Washington.* New York: American News Co., c. 1860.

Hough, Franklin B. *Washingtonia.* Vols. 1 and 2. Roxbury, Mass.: Privately published, 1865.

Hudson, J. Paul. *George Washington's Birthplace.* National Park Service Historical Handbook Series, No. 26, 1956 (reprinted 1961).

Hughes, Rupert. *George Washington.* Vols. 1 and 2. New York: William Morrow & Co., 1926-1927.

Hyde, Anna M. *Life of Washington.* New York: William L. Allison Co., c. 1860.

Irving, Washington. *Life of Washington.* Vols. 1-5. New York: G.P. Putnam & Co., 1855-1859.

Irving, Washington. *Life of Washington.* Vols. 1, 2, and 3. New York: R.F. Fenno & Co., 1900.

Johnson, Gerald W. and Wall, Charles Cecil. *Mount Vernon: The Story of a Shrine.* New York: Random House, 1953.

Kantor, MacKinlay. *Valley Forge.* New York: Ballantine Books, 1976.

Kent, Donald H. *Contrecoeur's Copy of George Washington's Journal for 1754.* Pennsylvania Historical and Museum Commission reprint, 1952.

Ketchum, Richard M. *The World of George Washington.* New York: American Heritage Publishing Co., 1974.

Kinnaird, Clark. *George Washington: The Pictorial Biography.* New York: Hastings House, 1967.

Kinnaird, Clark. *George Washington: The Pictorial Biography.* New York: Bonanza Books, 1967.

Kitman, Marvin. *George Washington's Expense Account.* New York: Simon & Schuster, 1970.

Knollenberg, Bernard. *George Washington.* Durham, North Carolina: Duke University Press, 1964.

Koral, Bella. *George Washington.* New York: Random House, 1954.

Lewis, Taylor, Jr., and Young, Joanne. *Washington's Mount Vernon.* New York: Holt, Rinehart & Winston, 1973.

Little, Shelby. *George Washington.* Garden City, New York: Halcyon House, 1943.

Lodge, Henry Cabot. *George Washington.* Vols. 1 and 2. Boston: Houghton Mifflin Co., 1898 (No. 365 or 500 printed).

Lossing, Benson J. *Mary and Martha: The Mother and the Wife of George Washington.* New York: Harper & Bros., 1886.

MacDonald, William. *George Washington: A Brief Biography.* Mount Vernon, Va.: The Mount Vernon Ladies Association of the Union, 1973.

McNeer, May. *The Story of George Washington.* Nashville & New York: Abingdon Press, 1973.

Mitchell, Lt. Col. Joseph B. *Decisive Battles of the American Revolution.* Greenwich, Conn.: Fawcett Publications, 1962.

89

Muir, Dorothy Troth. *Presence of a Lady, Mount Vernon, 1861-1868.* Mount Vernon, Va.: The Mount Vernon Ladies Association of the Union, 1975.

Muscalus, John A. *An Index of State Bank Notes That Illustrate Washington and Franklin.* Bridgeport, Pa., Privately published, 1938.

Nordham, George W. *George Washington: Vignettes and Memorabilia.* Philadelphia: Dorrance & Co., 1977.

Padover, Saul K. *The Washington Papers.* New York: Grossett & Dunlap, 1955.

Page, Edwin L. *George Washington in New Hampshire.* Boston & New York: Houghton Mifflin Co., 1932.

Page, Thomas Nelson. *Mount Vernon and Its Preservation.* Mount Vernon, Va.: The Mount Vernon Ladies Association of the Union, 1910.

Pier, Arthur. *The Young Man from Mount Vernon.* New York: Frederick A. Stokes Co., 1940.

Roberts, Allen E. *G. Washington: Master Mason.* Richmond, Virginia: Macoy Publishing & Masonic Supply Co., 1976.

Ryan, Dennis. *New Jersey in the American Revolution, 1763-1783 A Chronology.* New Jersey Historical Commission, 1974.

Schroeder, John Frederick. *Life and Times of George Washington.* Vol. 2. New York: Johnson Fry & Co., 1857.

Schroeder, John Frederick. *Maxims of Washington.* Mount Vernon, Va.: The Mount Vernon Ladies Association of the Union, 1942.

Schroeder-Lossing. *Life & Times of Washington.* Vols. 1, 2, and 3. Albany, N.Y.: M.M. Belcher Publishing Co., 1903.

Smith, James Morton, ed. *George Washington: A Profile.* New York: Hill & Wang, 1969.

Snell, Charles W., and Wilshin, Francis F. *Saratoga.* Washington, D.C.: National Park Service Historical Handbook Series, No. 4, 1950 (reprint 1961).

Stephenson, Nathaniel Wright and Dunn, Waldo Hilary. *George Washington.* Vols. 1 and 2. New York, London, Toronto: Oxford University Press, 1940.

Stevenson, Augusta. *George Washington: Boy Leader.* Indianapolis: Bobbs-Merrill Co., 1942.

Thane, Elswyth. *Potomac Squire.* Mount Vernon, Va.: The Mount Vernon Ladies Association of the Union, 1963.

Thane, Elswyth. *Mount Vernon Family.* New York: Crowell-Collier Press, 1968.

Townsend, Virginia F. *Life of Washington.* New York: Butler Bros., 1887.

Trussell, John B., Jr. *Epic on the Schuylkill: The Valley Forge Encampment 1777-1778.* Pennsylvania Historical and Museum Commission, 1974.

VanDyke, Paul. *George Washington: The Son of His Country.* New York: Charles Scribner's Sons, 1931.

Washburn, Mabel T.R. *George Washington.* New York: Samuel Gabriel Sons & Co., 1932.

Weems, Mason L., Jr. *A History of the Life and Death, Virtues and Exploits of General George Washington.* Philadelphia: J.B. Lippincott & Co., 1918.

Weems, M.L. *The Life of George Washington.* Philadelphia: J.B. Lippincott & Co., 1857.

Weig, Melvin J. *Morristown: A Military Capital of the American Revolution.* Washington, D.C.: National Park Service Historical Handbook Series, No. 7, 1950 (reprint 1961).

Wharton, Anne Hollingsworth. *Martha Washington.* New York: Charles Scribner's Sons, 1897.

Whipple, Wayne. *The Story-Life of Washington.* Vol. 2. Philadelphia: John C. Winston Co., 1911.

Wilbur, William H. *The Making of George Washington.* Available from Patriotic Education, Inc., DeLand, Florida. Second Edition, September, 1973.

Wilson, Woodrow. *George Washington.* New York: Schocken Books, 1969 (reprint of 1896 book).

Winthrop, Warren. *Exercises for Washington's Birthday.* Boston & Chicago: New England Publishing Co., 1892.

Wister, Owen. *The Seven Ages of Washington.* New York: Grossett & Dunlap, 1907.

Yaeger, Georgia A., and Kay, Robert J. *Washington Crossing State Park.* Albert A. Colacello, 1962.

American Heritage Book of Presidents and Famous Americans, The. Vol. 1. New York: American Heritage Publishing Co., 1967.

American Heritage Book of the American Revolution, The. New York: American Heritage Publishing Co., 1958.

General Washington's Military Equipment. Mount Vernon, Va.: The Mount Vernon Ladies Association of the Union, 1963.

George Washington Atlas, The. ed. Lawrence Martin. Washington, D.C.: United States George Washington Bicentennial Commission, 1932.

History of the George Washington Bicentennial Celebration, The. Vols. 1-5. Washington, D.C.: United States George Washington Bicentennial Commission, 1932.

Life of George Washington. Biographical School Series. Philadelphia: Lindsay & Blakiston, 1845.

Life of Washington—incomplete—c. 1860.

Messages and Papers of the Presidents (1789-1908). Vol. 1. Bureau of National Literature and Art, 1909.

Morristown National Historical Park. Washington Association of New Jersey, 1967.

Mount Vernon: An Illustrated Handbook. Mount Vernon, Va.: The Mount Vernon Ladies Association of the Union, 1974.

Speeches and Letters of George Washington. New York: Robert K. Haas, c. 1850.

About the Author

George W. Nordham is a graduate of George Washington University in Washington, D.C., and of the Law School of the University of Pennsylvania. He is a member of the Bar in the State of New York and in the District of Columbia.

His private collection of Washingtonia includes books, articles, paintings, busts, coins and medals, plates and plaques, cups, mugs, postage stamps, currency, trays, decanters, banks, thimbles— virtually any item that features or describes George Washington. Many of the items in this collection are described in Mr. Nordham's book *George Washington: Vignettes and Memorabilia.*